DESPERATE
SOCCER
MOMS
[AND DADS]

JEFF ILLINGWORTH

MW00810247

This book is dedicated to my two sons Danny and Ben.

Critical Acclaim for Jeff Illingworth

"Jeff had a tremendous impact on my soccer career, especially during my early pre-teen years. He introduced me to competitive soccer and helped provide ma opportunities for my future. Jeff's help, along with commitment and sacrifices my parents made, paved the way for a long enjoyable soccer career, which has shaped me as a person. These experiences include gaining a strong education and earning an MBA from the University of San Diego. With Jeff's high level training and contacts I was able to spend three summers in Manchester, England training and competing. This provided opportunities to develop lifelong friends and once in a lifetime experiences. Jeff and I have not always agreed on things, but I will always have respect for him and am grateful for our long-term relationship!"

> - Charles "Chugger" Adair
> *Associate Head Coach Virginia Tech Women's Soccer*
> *Co - Captain USD Men's Soccer 1991 and 1992*
> *NCAA Finalist 1992*
> *NCAA All - American 1992*
> *9 Year Professional Player*

"After more than 30 years working with coaches and athletes I can say that Jeff Illingworth is a very skillful coach, not just with tactics and strategies but specially understanding the soul of athletes and parents. You should read this wonderful book!"

> - Grande Abraço
> *Roberto Shinyashiki MD, PhD is a specialist in Sports Psychology*
> *and was the coach of Brazilian team at Sidney Olympics Games.*
> *Author of 14 books that have being sold 6.5 millions. Today he is*
> *working with 65 Olympic athletes preparing for London Olympic games.*

"Jeff Illingworth is one of the top youth soccer coaches in the USA. His soccer knowledge, teaching techniques and motivational skills are second to none. I owe much of my success at Stanford University's soccer program to Jeff teaching me the sound fundamentals of the game as a youth soccer player. I played for several clubs growing up under Jeff and he always managed to put together one of the most competitive teams in Southern California. This provided an opportunity to get great exposure and play at a very high level (traveling to Europe several times) from the age of 8 through high school. In addition, his great sense of humor made all the practices fun and rewarding. His book shows all his attributes and is a must read. Not just for soccer parents but for all who enjoy a great adventure."

> - TK Inbody
> *Co-Captain – Stanford University 1999 – NCAA Finalists in 1998*

"Jeff's book is an honest portrayal of the early days in youth soccer in the San Diego community. His book brought back fond memories and I found it to be very entertaining."

> - Mike Connerley
> *Tournament Director, San Diego Surf Cup*

Contents

Prologue

"Regrets I've had a few" My Way - Frank Sinatra

This book is non-fiction and gives a true and accurate account of my first fifteen years coaching youth soccer in San Diego. In certain instances, it has been necessary to change names, locations, or certain details to 'protect the innocent.' Ninety-nine percent of the book is as accurate as my memory could make it. My real birth name is Godfrey, not Jeff! I am sure you can understand why I changed it to 'Jeff' instead. With a nick name of 'God', we use to get hundreds of people turning up at my parents home in England every Sunday morning.

As I approach 60 years of age, I decided it was time to write down many of the events of my roller coaster life in America, since 1981. In hind sight, I see many mistakes and decisions I have made along the way. Given the chance I would go back and correct many of the wrongs and avoid many of the confrontational situations. I would be quicker to forgive and forget and would wish for the ability to always see both sides of an argument. There is no one in this book who I have any continuing dislike or animosity towards. I seriously hope my detractors and former enemies can forgive my failings and poor choices.

Even the kindest, gentlest person may sometimes weaken under the intense pressure created in certain youth soccer situations. One young English coach newly arrived in San Diego said "It's only coaching Football to kids, anybody can do that". Within twelve months he gave up his three teams and returned to England saying "I can't handle the parents". I have been fortunate to enjoy 27 years in the youth soccer world and wish to thank every parent and child I have come into contact with. To those I failed, I apologize. For those I helped, I thank you for the opportunity.

Jeff Illingworth

DESPERATE SOCCER FANS

A fanatical soccer fan is sitting in front of the television with his Manchester United scarf and sweater. After an hour of watching the game, screaming at the TV, totally ignoring his wife who stands up and screams at him,

"You love Manchester United more than you love me!!!"

Without taking his eyes from the game on TV the husband replies,

"I love Chelsea more than I love you."

Soccer humor is often biting and cynical, born of the intense feeling that this great game produces. Goalkeepers are especially vulnerable since they play in the most critical area of the field.

After a disastrous game where the goalkeeper let in four easy goals, the crowd was giving him serious abuse. Unable to deal with the continued criticism, as he left the field, the goalkeeper lost control of his emotions and dived in front of an oncoming bus and MISSED. Typical!

INTRODUCTION
Soccer Moms and Dads
Why Are They So Desperate?!

"It's all about the kids" is the often quoted statement of fact expressed by many soccer parents. In an ideal world, this would and should be true, as it would make life so much easier. Especially for the coach! This statement is in fact a platitude that parents often use before setting off on a long, vitriolic complaint to the coach. The major complaints parents carry against their child's coach relate to:

1. Playing time!
2. The position their child plays
3. Playing time!
4. How the coach talks to their child
5. Playing Time!
6. Training is too hard and intensive
7. Playing Time!
8. Training is not intensive enough
9. Playing Time!
10. Why doesn't my child start?

Hence the Desperate Mom and/or Dad, who is consumed on the sideline as they watch their child sit for much or all of the game. Is this Mom or Dad wrong for feeling upset, angry, frustrated? No! Is there an easy answer to solving this ongoing problem? No! The more the season goes on and the more the Desperate Parent seethes with what is now desperation, the worse the situation becomes.

A "cancer" is now potent in the team, and if more than one player's parent is of the same mindset, this may well lead to the beginning or formation of a --- Desperate Soccer Parents Coalition.

PROBLEM:
"Desperate Soccer Parents Coalition"

If you have 12 players on an eight-a-side team and four players are THE SUBS, you have the potential for one third of the team parents to form a Desperate Coalition, for mutual sympathy and support. Is this unreasonable? Absolutely not, and in many ways it is entirely understandable. Is it healthy for the team or the coach? No!

There are some understanding, "reasonable," parents who understand that in the biggest, toughest, most important game, playing all the players may not necessarily be what's best for the team. "What's best for the team" is open to many opinions and has been the subject of thousands of arguments. What I know, is that in any competitive soccer situation, there are bound to be "playing time" Desperate Parents. If they form a coalition of discontent, the coach and the team begin to fragment.

Sometimes the coalition is hidden from the coach for a period of time, or the group may be aggressive enough to confront him/her early on.

In any good soccer club, there should be rules, written information, and pre-season meetings to discuss the potential playing time rules during the upcoming season. Despite taking all these precautions, not long into the season, after the pre-season tournaments end, the seeds of discontent will already be circulating on the side-line.

In many cases, the unfortunate team manager is often dragged into the situation by the disgruntled coalition. Hopefully, the worst has not happened and one of the Desperate Coalition is in fact the team manager.

PROBLEM:
Unrealistic Ambition

Desperate Soccer Moms (and Dads)

It is hard to believe that a parent of an eight or nine year old youth soccer player could possibly be thinking about College Scholarships or playing in The Pros. They do! Youngsters who are enjoying playing with their friends in their local area are often moved to "premier" teams to give them a "better chance" to eventually get a College Scholarship, despite the fact that they are ten years away from graduation from High School! In Southern California, people travel large distances in their regular life and are willing to drive their children thousands of miles to play at the best clubs or teams.

Undoubtedly, great young players should want to play with other players of equal ability, but parents who are desperate to ensure College success for their children are incredibly premature and misguided. Between 8 and 18 years of age, youngsters develop in many different ways, and it is impossible to predict where a young player will be when they become teenagers and then young adults. As time goes by many young soccer "prodigies" are over-taken by some of their lesser peers. It is sad to see these parents who have committed themselves early to driving their child forward. When they eventually realize (some never accept) that their child is not even a "starter" in their own club team, the Desperate Parent (unrealistic ambitions) is a devastating sight to behold.

Often, their child loses interest in soccer due to the never ending pressure and demands of the overly intense parent (or parents). Many of these parents invest incredible time, emotion, and even their marriage and social life in and around their child's youth soccer career. This "blind ambition" is even more disturbing when the young player was never a "potential star" in anyone's eyes other than his or her parents. It is astounding to hear parents talk about their child as The Best Player on the Team, when the vast majority of the other parents and the coach barely rate the youngster as worth a starting position, on his or her own team.

PROBLEM:
The Out of Control Desperate Mom (and Dad)

Some soccer parents are simply unable to control their emotions while watching their child play during the game. Their lack of control comes in many different displays, all of which are sad and pathetic to watch.

Some parents complain that everything is always wrong. Every referee decision against the team of the Desperate Parent, brings loud shouts of disgust and disagreement. While I watch and listen to these parents, I am amazed how often they are totally wrong. I can never understand why parents who act and behave normally away from the soccer field completely change character when they arrive at the game. After one game when the Desperate Mom (and Dad) saw their daughter's team lose 8-0, they stormed over to the referee and said, "You were pathetic! You lost us the game!" I repeat – their team lost 8-0!

The behavior of these parents can and does lead to frightening physical confrontations between the parent and coach or between parents on opposing teams. At the end of one game, two fathers confronted each other on the field and proceeded to "Do Battle." One was a powerful American Dad, and the other an Asian gentleman, smaller and wiry. The players were terrified as the American Dad threw wild punches and the Asian Dad used his Kung-Fu technique. Eventually, other parents from each team managed to intervene and end the debacle.

Confrontations between angry parents and coaches are frequent, especially immediately after the game. A "24 hour rule" is advisable and should be applied, to allow tempers to calm down. One particularly nasty dad/coach incident blew up during the game when the dad stormed up to the coach demanding to know, "When is my son going on the field? I'm leaving. I can't stand watching you coach!" As the Desperate Dad started to leave, the coach ill-advisedly pushed the son and said, "You may as well go with your Dad." When the father saw the coach push his son, he lost all his control, ran over, and punched the coach in the face. The police were called and charges filed.

Parent/referee altercations are occurring at an alarming rate and is the main reason why so many referees stop doing the job. At one game, a Desperate Dad, well known for his lack of control, threw a soccer ball and hit the referee on the head. The same dad was also guilty of scratching the car of the head-coach (not mine for a change!) at his own club. These are a few frightening, disturbing, but unfortunately common incidents.

One of the most aggressive and vocal parents in my soccer club overstepped the mark and chose the wrong coach to insult. The dad was five feet, five inches tall and weighed about 140 pounds. The coach, who was a volunteer, was six feet, two inches tall and weighed about 220 pounds (a former F.B.I. agent with enormous hands). He was a great guy, quiet, polite, organized, and dedicated to the young players in his team.

The coach substituted the son of the "small dad," who responded loudly with, "You're the biggest f..ing jerk I have ever seen."

The coach seeming seemingly missed the remark or chose to ignore it. However, after the game, I looked over to the car park and noticed the foul-mouthed dad walking toward his car. At the same time, I saw my coach vault the fence, stride toward the parent, and lift him off the ground with one hand. The dad dangled helplessly as my coach made it abundantly clear regarding any further incidents. If it had not been so sad, it could almost have been a situation comedy.

PROBLEM:
The Desperate Mom (usually Dad) –
"A Soccer Coaching Expert"

Despite the fact that most American parents have never played soccer, it is incredible how many of them, mainly Dads, believe they know everything about the game – certainly more than the coach! They march up and down the sideline, giving a running commentary on the progress of the game. Naturally, they express the great things their child is doing out on the field. Second guessing the coach is a sophisticated technique developed by these "volunteer assistant coaches." If their team loses, they have all the answers and reasons to explain the loss! If the coach allows it, these "volunteer coaches" will pull players away and give them their "pearls of wisdom" advice. How often I hear a parent saying the player should dribble at the same moment the coach shouts "pass the ball." These Desperate Dads need strong coaches to stop the players from becoming distracted.

This "volunteer" coaching can be dangerous, when a parent starts to coach and criticize players in the team (other than their own, of course). How often these parents see little wrong with their own child, but many failings with their teammates.

I had one nine year old girl playing for me who was tall, gangly, a little awkward, but possessing great size, power and blazing speed. She scored many goals and occasionally ran over her own player – ACCIDENTALLY of course. She was invaluable to our team!!! Nevertheless, some parents of other players on the team were constantly denigrating this young girl, despite the fact that their own daughters were certainly not as valuable or physically talented. During one game, one of my "soccer expert" dads, famous for his loud mouth, was negatively "coaching" (out of my hearing). He was criticizing the play of our "steamroller" player loudly enough for the girl's father to hear. The next moment, I heard a loud disagreement. As the game progressed, I turned to see both fathers squaring up to each other, ready to fight. "A rule of the soccer jungle" applied to the opinionated father, who had a loud mouth and had become a soccer expert. He was totally unwilling to hear any criticism of his daughter and had ridiculously inflated opinions of the talent of his own children.

Note! The parent "soccer expert" will also be the one (or more than one!) who constantly criticizes the referee.

Coaches be aware – this parent will also attempt to listen to every pre-game, half-time, and post-game coach's talk – often nodding, giving tactic agreement. Unless the game is lost, then the "expert" will wear an expression of pain and dissatisfaction, waiting their time to explain to anyone who will listen to what went wrong!

PROBLEM:
Desperate Moms (and Dads) –
"My Kid"s a Forward"

For many parents, the coach playing their child in defense, is considered to be an insult, denigrating the player's ability. The glory position is the forward player who will get all the glory and becomes the star of the team. Besides goalkeeping, playing forward is the most difficult position on the field – usually outnumbered, often receiving the ball under pressure, and facing the wrong direction. Scoring goals is a gift few players possess, especially as they get older and defenders become more sophisticated. If the other team has great forwards, it would seem to make sense for the coach to have great defenders in order to stop them from scoring. It is not unusual for a Desperate Parent to take their child away from a team, if the coach will not listen to the "sage" advice of the "unbiased" parent. "My daughter was a 'goal machine' when she played in the recreation league," the parent modestly advises the coach. "I have tried your daughter at forward and the 'machine' was broken," responds a witty coach.

"My child loves to score goals!" boasted one parent. As they walked away importantly, one of my coaches, who had overheard the parent quipped, "Her son couldn't 'score' with a hooker in Las Vegas." Many of those parents look at the goal scorer on their child's team with barely concealed envy and jealously. Often, they complain of the "selfishness" of that successful goal scorer, despite the benefits the goal scorer brings to the team. Jealousy is a nasty, emotionally-charged word. No parent will admit, overtly or inwardly, that they are jealous of players on their own child's team. Unfortunately, it happens at every level of youth soccer – coaches beware!

Mission Bay Soccer Club (MBSC)
1981 – 1985;
The Beginning

Settling into our two bedroom apartment at the Oakwood Apartment complex in Pacific Beach, we both felt excitement and fear of the unknown. Our only friends were an English couple, Jan and Warwick, who worked nearby at a first class French restaurant, L'Escargot, in beautiful La Jolla. On our previous vacation visits, we discovered L'Escargot and enjoyed Jan and Warwick's company. Honestly, without their help and encouragement, we would never have had the courage to immigrate. In fact, it was Warwick who gave me the contact that was to provide the big opportunity for me to access youth soccer in San Diego. He put me in touch with another ex-pat Englishman, Jeff Bishop, who owned a soccer store called Soccer Man. Jeff Bishop was the perfect mentor for me. He was a small, energetic soccer fanatic who did not have his ego involved. He knew everything about the small but developing soccer scene in San Diego. Coming from the Midlands area of England, he was an Aston Villa fan, and his local youth soccer club was naturally named Villa.

Jeff ran several weeks of soccer camps for youngsters in Solana Beach, 12 miles north of Pacific Beach. He was kind enough to hire me to coach/teach at his camps and soon left me in charge so he could attend to his soccer store. I was amazed to see the interest and enthusiasm of these five to ten year old boys and GIRLS! Yes, to me it was stunning as I had never seen any girls play soccer in England. The involvement of the parents was also intriguing to me. Some of the parents stayed for the whole three hours to watch and nearly all returned in time to watch the final half-hour of Camp. Teaching soccer in England, it was rare to have almost any parents attend the after school games. Having taught for ten years in extremely poor areas in Manchester, it was also a cultural shock to see these very attractive California mothers in shorts, gym attire, and other enticing attire. I thoroughly enjoyed the Camp weeks and was disappointed when they ended.

With lots of spare time that I had never enjoyed in England, Pauline and I relaxed at the pool and Jacuzzi at our Oakwood Apartment. I ran daily on the oceanfront Boardwalk and started to play tennis.

Jeff Bishop offered to help me advertise for a soccer-coaching job by placing flyers in his soccer store. He also informed me that many children played soccer at Ski Beach Park, only five minutes away from my apartment. One afternoon I jogged down to Ski Beach and sure enough, there were several groups of boys practicing.

One group of older boys aged about 15 or 16 was unbelievably skilled, and I watched in amazement. Several of the groups were obviously Hispanic, but many were not. I had never seen or coached any Hispanic youth soccer players before this. Nearby, another group of younger boys took part in what was a poorly organized, ill-disciplined debacle. A short, heavy-set, bald man with huge Popeye calf muscles was joining in this session as though he was one of the children. The older, talented boys were being coached by a little man with a broad North of England accent. The name on their shirts said, La Jolla Nomads. Later that night, I phoned Jeff Bishop to ask about the La Jolla Nomads. He told me that the head coach of the Nomads was Derek Armstrong from Blackpool, England. He had been hired by a wealthy La Jolla businessman, Joe Hollow, who paid Derek's salary. I asked how many other soccer clubs had paid professional soccer coaches. The answer was zero! My hopes for making a living coaching soccer seemed to be totally misguided and futile.

After weeks of tennis, swimming and running on the boardwalk, I was getting bored and wanted to get working again.

Similar to my good fortune years earlier getting a break into show business, Lady Luck was about to smile on me again. The phone rang, and when I answered it, an American voice asked to speak to Jeff Illingworth. "That's me. Can I help you?" I replied.

"Hi Jeff. My name is Hank Berthaume, and I saw your flyer in the Soccer Man store. I run a club called Mission Bay, and I may be interested in hiring a professional coach for some sessions." Fortunately, Hank lived only a few hundred yards away from my apartment, and even more pleasing, his club trained at Ski Beach!

I met Hank for lunch at a restaurant on the ocean front in Pacific Beach. Fate had played its hand. He was a short, bald, heavy-set man with huge, Popeye calf muscles! He was the same gentleman I had seen prancing around with the out of control younger boys recently at Ski Beach. We met for several hours, and finally Hank offered to hire me for 6 two hour sessions at $50 a session. He informed me that he had started Mission Bay Soccer Club a couple of years earlier. He had five boys' teams, ranging from Under 10 (U/10) through Under 16 (U/16). He basically organized and ran everything, including the Mission Bay Soccer Classic Tournament, held annually at Easter. I was excited to accept the coaching work but uneasy remembering the shambles I had seen a few days earlier.

The afternoon of my first coaching session arrived, and I waited patiently for the players to arrive for our 3:30 practice. Slowly the disinterested boys arrived. They were dressed in an array of beach shorts, sneakers, brightly colored t-shirts, and had a total lack of enthusiasm. By about 3:45, I had eleven players and tried to get them organized and listening. Hank's attempts to get order were totally ignored. After ten years of teaching in two of England's toughest areas, I was in no mood to be beaten by a group of young California beach boys.

"I'll give twenty dollars to anyone who can dribble the ball past me and score a goal!" I offered. Silence followed with eleven sets of eyes staring in my direction. "Get a ball each and line up at that cone in five seconds to get a chance," I ordered. Suddenly ten young boys were scurrying to get a ball and line up. The eleventh jogged towards the goal with a smile on his face. "Does that include me?" Hank smirked. "Yes, $50 if you can dribble past me and score," I replied, determined that not even with a miracle of luck would my chunky "employer" get anywhere near a goal.

For 15 minutes the boys and Hank tried and failed, with Hank looking more frustrated than the boys! He had little idea of how to play and had a peculiar running style - high up on his toes with his arms bent, swinging just under his chin. In England, his running style would have tagged him as a "Woofter." (effeminate)

Part way through the practice, another boy arrived on a beach bicycle wearing huge, wet, beach shorts and dripping wet hair. By now I had the attention of the group and was none too pleased by the interruption of this late comer. Seemingly oblivious to me, the youngster started to laugh and joke with Hank and the other players, totally disrupting the session. "Who are you?" I demanded in an unfriendly voice. "I'm an American. WHAT are you?" came back the sassy reply from the 14 year old. Hank and the other players were enthralled by the "verbal battle." Inwardly, I smiled, thinking how much this kid reminded me of myself as a youngster.

Darren Fanelli was his name, and during the next few years we were to become great friends and mutually supportive in helping Mission Bay Soccer Club develop and prosper.

It was clear during the remainder of the practice that Darren was a very good soccer player, great athlete, and the "spiritual leader" of that team.

At the end of the first session, finishing with a decent scrimmage, the players were friendly as they left with their parents. Another new experience for me was to see all the cars arrive to ferry their sons home. In England, most of the boys walked home or used the bus (public transportation).

Hank seemed pleased with what had happened during the session, but refused when I asked him if he wanted to go to the local bar, Rocky's, for a beer. He was not married, had no children of his own, but I was to discover he was somewhat of a loner.

I went to watch several of the Mission Bay teams play over the next few Saturdays. All of the teams had one common denominator – lack of discipline. Hank's attempts to coach were futile, and he was totally ignored by his own players. I was itching to jump in, but was wary of undermining Hank.

As the six coaching sessions came to an end, Hank told me of his Mission Bay Classic Soccer Tournament with over two hundred teams. In the early 1980's, this was a big deal. I was thrilled when he offered to hire me as Head Coach for the remaining eight months of the season. I would be paid $1100 per month for coaching all five teams twice a week and on Saturday game days. Although my relationship with Hank would eventually go horribly wrong, this great opportunity he gave me can never be forgotten. Without this, I may well have been living back in England within a year.

Through another lead, I found a part time job teaching Physical Education in a small private Catholic school in nearby Ocean Beach. Sacred Heart School was small, with about 200 boys and girls aged 5 – 14 years, and a huge church at the end of the street. The Monsignor Rattigan was a surly, taciturn gentleman who asked for my Green Card information to verify my legal status in the USA. A major problem! I told him I was in the process of getting a work permit. With 30 days to spare before my teaching was to begin, I found an attorney, Lyn Ceithaul, who quickly got me an H1 temporary work permit, which I proudly showed to Mr. Happy - Monsignor Rattigan. One thing that really pissed me off was that he was Irish – not even American!

Now with two jobs again – just like my life in England – I felt that I was making progress. Unlike my life in England, I did not have to drive hundreds of miles at night and arrive home after midnight. My coaching was 3:30 – 7:00 PM, Monday through Friday, and my teaching was 8:00 AM to noon, Monday through Friday. Pauline was getting regular work as a substitute teacher, using her social security card acquired legally years earlier when she had dated an American who lived in Cleveland. Despite the social security card, Pauline was still not legally entitled to work. Years later, her "illegal status" was to become a huge asset!

Over the next eight months, I worked hard to instill discipline, organization, and fitness into all five teams. Hank was a dedicated, hard worker, but his relationship with all the boys was more like a cuddly big brother.

Throughout the eight months of the season, one big learning curve I had to overcome was refereeing. Because so few people in San Diego in 1981 had any real soccer experience, it makes sense that the number of qualified, competent referees would be few and far between. With 27 years of hindsight, I should have been much more phlegmatic and understanding. In 1981, I was frustrated, angry, and all too often out of control. If a Green Card had been as easy to get as a Red Card, I would have been legal within a week!

Not only were most of the referees incompetent, they were often arrogant, acted superior, and behaved as if they were the Main Event. Then I found out that they were paid for every game, I was under serious threat of exploding with a brain hemorrhage!

One game, I received a Red Card BEFORE THE GAME BEGAN! My team of seven year olds was warming up. I gave the game ball to the huge referee, who proceeded to press his thumbs down on the ball using all of his considerable weight. With 300 pounds of downward pressure, inevitably the ball compressed somewhat.

"Too soft – change it," ordered the referee.

"Too soft for what?" I asked angrily.

"Too soft to play the game, coach – change it."

I picked up a nearby ball, which was too hard and said, "Try heading that ref," as I tossed it toward him. The ref stood there, immobile, as the ball flew toward him. Obviously, he had never headed a ball in his life. With his hands already employed holding the "soft ball," the incoming ball hit him in the face. Not only did he not head the ball, he didn't even duck down to avoid it. He was furious!

"Assault of a ref!" he screamed. Frantically searching his pockets for the Red Card, he finally brandished it as he glared at me.

I didn't know whether to laugh or cry as Hank ran over

to see what all the fuss was about. In 2008, I still have the same issues with referees as to how hard a soccer ball should be for younger teams. My approach nowadays is to ask, "Ref, please give me one benefit of using a hard ball and one negative of using a softer ball?"   Sometimes it works - sometimes it doesn't. Kids hate playing with a rock hard soccer ball.

"Isn't Living in the USA Dangerous?"

When Pauline and I told our family and friends we had decided to move to live in San Diego, USA, we received some concerned responses. Several of our friends viewed America as a dangerous place to live due to the large number of people who owned guns. Certainly on British TV, there were regular news reports of shootings and occasional mass-murders shown to occur in the USA. On our several vacations to the US, we had not seen any violence or crime and felt comfortable about our decision to settle in San Diego.

Several months after beginning my coaching at Mission Bay Soccer Club, Pauline and I were invited to a house party at the home of the parents of one of my players. At the party, the host parents introduced us to a couple who were friends of theirs and similar in age to my wife and I. Also, neither of us had any children, and all four of us were athletic and interested in exercise. We immediately warmed to this couple who extended an invitation to us to visit their home for a barbeque the next weekend. I was pleasantly surprised at how many contacts and opportunities were opening up through my coaching career.

The following week we drove to Kensington, a delightful area of houses with great charm near downtown San Diego. Our new friends welcomed us warmly and showed us around their tastefully decorated artistic home. They were very talented artists who made a good living producing renderings of large construction projects. The husband, Gary, did the incredibly detailed drawings and his wife, Corrine, finished off with the coloring of the drawings. We had a wonderful evening and were treated to superb steaks and great wine. For Pauline and me, it was a huge step forward in settling into our new lifestyle.

We arranged to meet Gary and Corrine the next day at a hotel on Mission Bay. I would play tennis with Gary, and Pauline would run around the Bay with Corrine. I thoroughly enjoyed my tennis game, although I lost narrowly to Gary who was a solid player. Our wives arrived back from their run sweating and in good spirits. We all enjoyed the Jacuzzi and had a great meal at the hotel restaurant.

I was intrigued looking at our new friends and studying the dynamics of their relationship. She was unabashedly the one in charge, and clearly Gary was a quiet gentleman, content to defer to his wife. Corrine was confident, intelligent, and extremely opinionated. Gary was quick to smile, easy going, and easy to like. Over the following months, the four of us spent a great deal of time socializing together. It was interesting to me to note how they literally spent 24 hours a day in each other's company. They seemed a perfect couple with their own business, athletic lifestyle, and energetic personalities.

Pauline and I were delighted to be invited to visit them at their "winter home" in Alpine Meadows at Lake Tahoe. We spent a memorable week there, rafting down the Truckee River, hiking, playing tennis, and enjoying quiet dinners at their beautiful mountain home.

As the months passed, I began to find Corrine somewhat overbearing, and gradually our friendship began to dissolve, albeit in an amicable way. About a year later, we were walking around Mission Bay and by chance we met Gary and Corrine. They told us they had bought a new home in La Jolla and had sold their house in Kensington. We wished each other well and went our separate ways.

A year later, driving through La Jolla, I saw Gary driving a convertible Mercedes SL sports car – top down – but no Corrine. I thought it unusual when I spotted him again – on his own – driving through Pacific Beach. I mentioned it to Pauline and idly wondered if there had been a problem in the relationship between our former friends.

The answer came in a devastating way. Reading the local community newspaper, The La Jolla Light, I saw the front page headline – "Local Man Murders Wife and Commits Suicide." As I read the names of the dead couple, I was heartbroken to read Gary and Corrine!

Corrine had returned to their La Jolla home after they had separated from each other to pick up some of her belongings. Inexplicably, Gary had lost control and had bludgeoned Corrine to death. He then shot himself. With tears in my eyes, I silently handed the newspaper to my wife. A few seconds later, I heard her scream and collapse onto a chair. We were both speechless and frightened. This loving, committed couple with a vibrant, successful lifestyle were both dead. The words of our English friends were to spring to mind, "Isn't living in the USA dangerous?"

Trying to rationalize this tragic event, we tried to comfort each other with the belief that it was a freak incident which would never happen again to anyone we knew.

We hoped for this, but the future was to prove us horribly wrong.

MBSC – First Success

As eight months flew past, we arrived at the Easter Holiday and The Mission Bay Soccer Classic Tournament. Hank had worked hard, and the Tournament included many teams from other cities and a few from other states. Only two years before, I had brought my boys all-star team from Salford, England to the Dallas Cup Tournament. My experience in Dallas was not a total success.

The Dallas Cup was, and still is, one of America's and the World's top youth soccer tournaments. I was intrigued by the Dallas Cup and now the Mission Bay Classic Tournament. In Britain, "The Birthplace of Soccer," there were no tournaments similar to these two great events. I was beginning to realize already that America may not treat soccer as a "religion," but the ability and capacity to promote and organize it was already in place.

My Mission Bay U/16 boy's team had arrived back a few weeks earlier from their high school soccer season. We had trained hard and were determined to do well in our own tournament. Darren Fanelli had even offered to give up staying out all night, avoid alcohol and smoking "the weed" – true dedication for a 14 year old – our youngest player!

As the Mission Bay Classic Tournament progressed, our goalkeeper, John Mazur, was spectacular. We tied, or beat teams who were undoubtedly better than us. Darren's "lifestyle change" had resulted in his undoubted talent being fully realized. This little guy was a thorn in the side of all our opponents. He led by example and we fought our way forward game by game. Amazingly, we made the final, and we were all buzzing, waiting for our afternoon game against a "team of thugs" from Las Vegas.

Hank was in a state of shock. No Mission Bay team

had ever won a league or a tournament. He tried to give me a million or more "coaching hints," on tactics, formation, and motivation for the Big Game.

"Thanks Hank. You make sure the Tournament keeps going well and I'll do my best to win it," I admonished. I was surprised how nervous I was myself, not realizing that a good result would propel me into "hero status" and a long term future with the Club.

Before the game, I took Darren aside and told him to keep his cool when the big Las Vegas defenders started to foul and kick him. He was up for the game and looked confident and focused.

The game began and the atmosphere was highly charged with many of our younger players and their parents there to support their club. I reflected on my many games coaching school teams in England over my ten-year teaching career. None compared with the intense buzz and excitement I felt as the game progressed. The Las Vegas team was supremely confident and played a physical game, like an English team getting "stuck in." My boys were inspired, playing bravely with great organization and discipline. In the six months since joining Mission Bay Soccer Club, those were the two aspects of team play I had emphasized time and again, slowly seeing progress.

The game ebbed and flowed on a knife edge, with both teams testing the opponent's goalkeeper. Our goalkeeper John was a talented player with great natural goalkeeping ability, and he showed all of it in this game. They shot and hit our crossbar, they shot and John made an amazing save. At the other end, Darren was involved in an ongoing David and Goliath battle, fighting for every ball sent in his direction. The longer the game went, the confidence of the Las Vegas team seemed to dissolve and slip away, and my players grew in confidence and belief. The game ended in a tie, and after a nail-biting overtime, we headed into a penalty shootout – something I had never seen or experienced. I glanced along the touchline, taking in what was now a huge throng of hundreds of spectators and players. I tried to appear calm, but my stomach was knotted, and I felt more nervous than on my first show business appearance.

After five penalties each, we were tied – 3 scores and 2 misses. We missed our sixth penalty and they only had to score on their next try to win the Tournament. We had given our all and I was proud of my boys. The big Las Vegas defender, about to take the penalty, waved back at his team with a big smile on his face. Arrogant bastard! I prayed that if nothing else, he would miss. He struck the ball ferociously and started to turn away to celebrate. Our goalkeeper flew across the goal and incredibly tipped the ball against the post, rebounding to safety. Tied again, my seventh kicker scored and the Las Vegas player couldn't handle the pressure and shot his ball wide. We were the Mission Bay Classic Champions! There was hugging, screaming, kissing, and tears as pandemonium broke out. A team that had finished near the bottom of its own league, had beaten one of Nevada's premier teams! It was my proudest moment in 12 years of teaching and coaching.

That night, my wife and I arrived at L'Escargot restaurant with me carrying a huge trophy. Our friends who worked there, were thrilled to hear the news, and Warwick gave us one of his special margaritas blended with the white of an egg – fabulous!

Shortly after arriving at the restaurant, I was astounded to see a young, Middle Eastern gentleman and a gorgeous young lady enter, flanked by bodyguards. Warwick quietly informed us that he was the grandson of one of the kings of a large oil producing country. He was living in

San Diego, studying at United States International University. As fate would have it, he was a huge soccer fan and was sponsoring the soccer program at the university. He asked about the trophy and found enough money to generously buy us a round of drinks to celebrate my success.

Shortly after they left, Warwick invited us to try some of the wine they had not used. At $500 a bottle we were ecstatic. Also interesting was to watch their payment of the bill. Cash only! One of the bodyguards opened a briefcase which was full of $100 bills. They left a $400 tip and disappeared quietly out of the restaurant. What a day it had been – life in America was taking shape!

The week following the Mission Bay Tournament win, I was to once again receive a lesson in the cultural and legal differences between life in California and England.

My Under 18 boy's team was coming to the end of their season. Every Thursday evening I would meet them on the oceanfront boardwalk in South Mission Beach. We would all do a five mile training fitness run together. I lived across the boulevard on the bay, a hundred yards away.

I mentioned to Hank how much I had enjoyed coaching this group of young men and would be sorry to say goodbye to them. Most of them were high school seniors who would be heading off to college in the coming months. I told Hank that I planned to have a "farewell party" for my players, and I would provide the food and beer for everybody. We would hold the party on the beach outside of my apartment. My wife, Pauline, and I had moved on from Oakwood and rented a two-bedroom upstairs apartment looking across the bay to Sea World.

When Hank heard of my plans, he nearly choked. "You must be joking. Most of the players are only 17 years old and the rest are 18!" he shouted.   Many of my players were taller than me, some had moustaches – one had a beard – and several of them looked to be in their twenties. Young men.

"What harm would a couple of beers do to them?" I asked.

"Firstly, the legal age for drinking alcohol is 21! Secondly, most of these guys drive cars and will be driving themselves home. Thirdly, the police beach patrol would certainly I.D. your players when they see them drinking beer. You would certainly go to jail and be kicked out of the country for corrupting minors!" Hank was in a state of panic. Within three months, my inexperience and naiveté of American morality, laws, and levels of acceptable behavior had twice put me in real danger of catastrophe.

"So these young men don't drink any alcohol until they are 21 years of age?" I asked incredulously.

"Of course they do. They all drink regularly, and many of them smoke "pot." However, they do it all in the privacy of home parties, and they supply or provide their own liquor and drugs," Hank said nonchalantly.

"What a load of bollocks! They are old enough to go to war but they can"t have a beer," I replied.

"Deal with it. You are living in America, not England," Hank warned.

In 2008, I still feel the same. The hypocrisy of forcing 18, 19, and 20 year olds who can vote but have to hide and drink alcohol only at private parties and in remote areas.

The season ended and Hank offered me a deal for the following season - $1,200 a month for a ten month season. I was thrilled and delighted to accept.

My relationship with Hank was strange and interesting. I was to meet many people in subsequent years who volunteered many hours, but had no children of their own in the program. Hank was single but had no girl friends or close male friends. He had no other hobbies or interests. He made a living repairing auto equipment, running his own one-man business. He did not go out to bars or night clubs, dressed very casually all the time, and dedicated himself totally to Mission Bay Soccer Club. I was very fortunate to have stumbled on this situation. He seemingly volunteered all his time and expertise for free, and appeared willing to use some of the profits from the Tournament to pay my salary. We shook hands, and I looked forward to the tryouts for the forthcoming season.

During the vacation, I worked for a soccer camp director named Mike Hovenic who ran a series of well organized soccer camps all over San Diego County.

It was at one of these camps that I discovered my first "franchise" player. Tall, slim and quiet, this boy possessed superb soccer skills and incredible maturity. He was nine years old and had a great nickname. "Chugger" Adair, was to be a cornerstone of MBSC for the next few years. His real name, Charles, had given way to Chugger because of his voracious appetite as a young child. Despite major operations as a young child for a serious hole in his heart, he was able to play hard every minute of every game. I bonded with this boy and enjoyed meeting his mother Ginger throughout the week of the camp. On Friday, Ginger asked me if I would be interested in Chugger playing for me at Mission Bay. I was stunned! They lived in Chula Vista, close to the Mexican Border. To play for me would require a 50 mile round trip, twice a week for practice and again on Saturday game day. This was to be the first of many amazing commitments from mothers and fathers, who were willing to drive vast distances, to enable their child to play for a specific team or coach. In England, most players played in their own neighborhood and games were usually within a few miles.

In addition to "Chugger," my school teaching job enabled me to "scout" prospective players from the Ocean Beach area during my physical education lessons. Jon Frichtel was a gifted athlete and excellent soccer player, the same age as Chugger, and I convinced him and his parents to join MBSC. He then brought his friend, Nelson Medina, who was to eventually play at the National level. Almost overnight, I had a quality under 10 boy's team with three superb players.

Bakersfield – Oil, Cotton and Soccer Opportunity!

Hank had arranged for us to take some of our teams to a tournament in a town north of Los Angeles called Bakersfield. Although the butt of many jokes and negative comments, Bakersfield was to become a huge source of income and players for me.

Driving the last hour into Bakersfield, across a flat, boring landscape, with the dank air and swirling mist. I did not relish the next three days of the upcoming tournament. The next day was miserable as I coached the games with strands of cotton blowing in the wind. Despite the depressing weather and unhealthy air, the soccer games were exciting and competitive. Chugger's team was playing great soccer and grabbing the attention of many coaches, parents, and players from other teams.

On the last day of the tournament, my under 10 boy's team were in the final against a strong Bakersfield team. Chugger had scored a total of ten goals, supported by great play from Jon and Nelson and the rest of the team. The field was surrounded by hundreds of spectators as the final began. It was obvious to me that the Bakersfield boys were less skilled, but were playing with great passion and aggression. We played quality soccer but struggled to score. Against the run of play, they scored on a long, hopeful shot. Their supporters went crazy. The atmosphere increased as we attempted to equalize. With just seconds left in the half, Chugger almost casually dribbled past four defenders and calmly rolled the ball into the corner of their goal. Eery silence! Half-time arrived. In the second half, Chugger scored again and inexorably we took charge of the game and ended up winning comfortably.

After the game, Hank introduced me to two men who were brothers, who lived in Bakersfield and were actively involved in youth soccer. Julian and Gerry Goodell were in awe of the soccer skills of my under 10 teams. They asked if I would be willing to run some week-long soccer camps in Bakersfield. They assured me that they could provide a minimum of 40 kids per camp at $100 per player. America, the land of opportunity! $4,000 a week in 1982 was huge money. Bakersfield suddenly looked more like "Paradise Found."

Bakersfield Soccer Camps – Opportunity Beckons

True to their promise, the Goodells set up two soccer camps for me at Bakersfield College. With more than forty children in each camp, I was ecstatic and brought in friends of mine to work the camps and "socialize" with me at night. What wasn"t so exciting was the 105 degree heat we faced every day. The local kids never complained and showed a real, honest work ethic. The camp ran from 8:00 AM to 2:00 PM Monday through Friday. Many of the youngsters were lacking in basic skills, but there were several outstanding players. Two Hispanic brothers, Ruben and Rudy Rosales were very talented, and a very gifted and small boy named Charlie Lynch was also exceptional. How I wished these three lived 225 miles away in San Diego!

During the week, I became good friends with the parents of the Rosales brother. Ruben Sr. and Frances were wonderful people who owned a burger and pie restaurant in downtown Bakersfield called " Happy Jacks." I started to joke about the name because Ruben Sr., although a great guy, was a "prophet of doom" – if he bought a toy dog, it would die! When I visited "Happy Jacks," I couldn't stop laughing when I read the large sign above the counter:

"We absolutely reserve the right to refuse service to ANYBODY" – signed HAPPY JACK!!!

At the end of a great camp week, in the heat, my three friends from England - Steve, Dave and Phil - and myself happily headed back on a four-hour drive to spend the weekend in San Diego. In addition to making great money, I had made several good, new friends in Bakersfield. The four of us had been invited to several families' homes and BBQs.

The four of us reluctantly left beautiful, warm, sunny

Mission Bay and headed back on the long journey to Bakersfield for Week 2 of Jeff Illingworth Soccer Camps. Seeing all the Bakersfield kids wearing camp t-shirts with my name on the front gave me a great feeling of achievement. In less than two years since arriving, jobless, in the USA, I was now Head-Coach of a thriving Club – Mission Bay – physical education teacher at a great little Catholic private school, and now Director of my own soccer camps!

In Bakersfield I noted again the enormous involvement and commitment of many of the soccer parents. Myself and my three coaches were treated like "heroes" bringing "The Good Word to the Needy." My staff was thrilled to be offered numerous opportunities to party and socialize with the Bakersfield mothers. One potentially difficult incident arose, when one of my coaches was socializing with one of the mothers of a girl, from our soccer camp. Unfortunately, her husband had arrived back a day early from a business trip. By shear chance, he stopped in the same bar for a quick drink. Six-foot two, "muscles in his spit," and ferocious looking, he sauntered toward my coach and his wife.

When his wife saw him, she was somewhat taken aback and the best she could do was –

"Hi Bill! This is our daughter's soccer-camp coach from England." Short and sweet, but hardly a valid excuse for being in a bar at 9:30 in the evening with another man's wife.

Amazingly, the words "English soccer-camp coach" seemed to reassure the giant, before he ripped my coach to pieces (or my coach ran and dived out of the windows of the bar).

This would not be the last of the "near escapes" for my coaching staff over the next 25 years.

It reminds me of the story of the soccer-coach in bed

with a desperate soccer mom, when he heard the front door open.

"Who's that?" he asked.

"My husband!" she replied.

"You said you were divorced!" he said, in panic.

"I lied," she answered.

"Where is your emergency exit?" he demanded.

"We don't have one," she answered.

"Where would you like one!" he hissed as he jumped out of the bed.

The second week of camp was going well, but staying out late with my three mates, then facing six hours in the blazing Bakersfield sun, was a challenge every morning.

Dave Ricketts was working for me while he was on leave from his teaching job in the United Arab Emirates. A true Cockney (London) accent and a dry sense of humor, he had some great stories about life in the Middle East. On his first day in Sharjah, UAE, he had taken his students out onto the concrete playground, telling them to do a set of pushups. No problem except it was 111 degrees and the concrete was sizzling. Also a slight problem was the fact that one of the students was the grandson of the ruler of the Country!!

Dave introduced us to the kids sing-along song - Heads and Shoulders, Knees and Toes - which he performed at the Camp. His one difficulty was caused by his inability to touch his toes because of a protruding beer belly!

During the week, one of the parents invited us to dine at his upscale (yes, Bakersfield has some) restaurant. The clientele was nicely dressed, and the four of us dressed in jackets, slacks, and shirts. Toward the end of the meal, the noise level was a low buzz, controlled, conservative atmosphere. I told Dave to get ready. I walked out into the middle of the restaurant and loudly clinked a spoon on a saucer to gain attention of all the diners. Somewhat surprised, slowly all of the crowd stopped talking and looked in my direction. "Ladies and gentlemen, tonight we have a special guest entertainer, direct from the Middle East. Please welcome . . . Dave Ricketts!" Somewhat reluctantly, the applause began as Dave took my place in the middle of the restaurant. Standing ramrod straight, hands at his side, he stared straight out in front of him, with a serious, fixed expression. As soon as the applause stopped, he slowly raised his hands to his head and started to sing slowly in his Cockney accent, "Heads and shoulders …" The faces of the audience will be in my memory forever. They didn't know whether to laugh or cry! Gradually some began to realize it was a spoof, and with me, Steve and Phil joining in, the crowd caught the mood and 150 adults in downtown Bakersfield were singing Heads and Shoulders Knees and Toes.

At the end of the second camp week, I was feeling sorry to leave our new friends, the Rosales Family. My next learning curve was about to arrive as we all hugged each other goodbye. Ruben Sr. (Happy Jack) asked me if I would be interested in his two sons playing for me at Mission Bay Soccer Club. I was dumbfounded! The round trip journey from Bakersfield to San Diego was 470 miles! I asked how often they would be able to play for me in San Diego. "Every week," Ruben Sr. answered simply.

For the next four years, Ruben Sr., Frances, Ruben Jr. and Rudy would make the enormous trek to San Diego, leaving home at 3:00 AM Saturday morning if there was an 8:00 AM kick off. If there was also a Sunday game, they would stay the night in a hotel and return to Bakersfield late Sunday evening. They were, and still are, a fabulous family who still own and manage Happy Jacks – Best

Burgers and Pies in Bakersfield. Both boys eventually received soccer scholarships to Fresno State and are now happily married with a family of their own. Where did those 25 years go?!?

Despite their incredible sacrifice and the enormous talent of this wonderful family, I still remember my shock and disgust when two disgruntled sets of parents in La Jolla stopped me after a game in San Diego to express their "displeasure" and "anger" that "their sons practiced twice a week and rarely started in most games."

"Why should the Bakersfield boy start every game and play all the time when he never practices during the week? " the first mother asked. "It sucks!"

"Yes, it's not fair!" offered the other mother vehemently.

Both dads, standing a couple of paces back nodded in unison.

"Because the boy is a genius! The family drives 470 miles and they wake up at 3:00 AM every Saturday to drive down here. The team is so much better with him in the line-up."

My answer fell on deaf ears. In truth, I made no attempt to placate or cajole the two sets of Desperate parents. Probably, because I didn't like any of them personally, and their sons were weaker players, with "weaker personalities."

Yet again, I (Mr. Diplomacy!) had managed to piss off four wealthy parents who were influential members of the affluent La Jolla community.

I had still not read the book, How to Make Friends and Influence People. The four parents strode away seemingly unconvinced by my "snappy" reply.

"Another door closes!"

Year Two and Three – MBSC – Expansion – Onwards and Upwards

With the Club expanding rapidly, Hank and I agreed that we needed an extra coach. I particularly was not comfortable with Hank's well meaning attempts at game day coaching on Saturdays. We now had nine teams, and our reputation as a serious soccer club was growing rapidly. Our neighbors, the La Jolla Nomads, had a National reputation, but in the younger ages, we were beginning to compete with them.

After several discussions, Hank agreed that I could contact an old college friend of mine, Joe. He was the Head of the Department of Physical Education in Salford, England. I had taught two miles away from him and was an admirer of him as a great guy and a first class teacher/coach. Physically, Joe was not an imposing sight; standing 5'5", bald, with horrendous eye-sight and glasses, straggly moustache and beard, duck feet, strange walk and a caustic, dry sense of humor. During our college days together, Joe was asked about his premature baldness. "Just unlucky I suppose. It's hereditary. My mother and sisters are all bald," he replied dryly. For obvious reason, Joe was single. Several years before, he'd had a girlfriend, but it ended when she beat him up in a fight. He liked the idea of coming to America, and eight weeks later he landed in San Diego with a broad smile on his face.

Tryouts were a success, and we readied ourselves for the forthcoming season. One evening, a lady approached me and said she wanted her son to play for our team. He was eight years old. I told her that our eight year old team was already full, and we would only consider a superstar, who was the best player in San Diego. Looking me straight in the eye, she replied quickly,

"Great! He is a superstar and he is the best player in San Diego!"

"Oh really. When can I see him?" I asked sarcastically.

"Now. He is in the car," she answered jogging athletically toward a huge car.

She returned with the classic, California, All American kid – blond hair, blue eyes, sparking teeth, and a Hollywood smile. I couldn't help myself!

"Well, he will look great on the team photo if nothing else," I quipped. The humor was lost.

"Yes, he will," replied the mother.

I passed the ball to the youngster and asked him to dribble past me. He did! Standing casually, I stuck out a foot to steal the ball from him. He cut one way, and as I tried to recover, changed direction and went past me. Lucky little sod! Next time I defended correctly and he still got me moving the wrong way, but he didn't have the speed to go past me! Oh yes, he was only eight years old!

"Franchise Player" number 2 had arrived at Mission Bay soccer club. TK Inbody - a gift from heaven, dropped in my lap. With Darren Fanelli as my original "Franchise Player," leading the older group, the club was beginning to take shape.

My Assistant Coach and long time friend, Joe, was temporarily living with Pauline and me, so my social life took on an extra dimension. Joe was an avid golfer, and we started to play Torrey Pines Golf Course, home to the 2008 U.S. Open. One day after the end of the Buick Open at Torrey Pines, we were playing the Course with hordes of others. With two strangers as partners, Joe, with his straggly beard and moustache, and me waited patiently with twelve other golfers on the par 3 sixth hole. We were joined by another foursome, making a very crowded tee of 16. The new foursome wore clothes and hats with Texas emblems. In a broad Texan accent, a big guy with a ten-gallon hat asked,

"Have you guys been waiting long?" Twelve sets of eyes looked at him incredulously. Quick as a flash, Joe answered,

"I was clean shaven when I came on this tee." Everybody exploded in fits of laughter.   Oh yes – the round took six and one half hours! Welcome Joe to the USA.

Joe – Learning a New Way of Life and New Language

Although Coach Joe had taught soccer in English school for 12 years, he had never really done soccer drills or coached a team on a regular long-term basis. In English school, Physical Education game lessons were basically, pick teams and play for an hour. Because of poor weather, no children wanted to sit around. Often the soccer had to be played indoors in the gymnasium. Joe needed to watch me, to pick up an array of drills, which I had created or copied, from other coaches at other clubs or from videos.

Another problem was the extreme difference in meaning of certain words which could be somewhat embarrassing. When I asked children to "shag the balls," Joe nearly collapsed in embarrassment. The word "shag" in England is the crudest slang word for sexual intercourse. It would not be long before Joe ran afoul of the principle "England and the US; two countries separated by the same language." Trying to motivate one of our Mission Bay older teams, Joe admonished one of the players who avoided a tackle. "You can't win if you play like a pussy!" Rarely do you see a group of 17 year old California young men tongue tied in a state of shock.

In private, I explained to Joe that in the USA vernacular, the word "pussy" was used to describe a woman's private parts. Usually phlegmatic, he blushed, stuttered, shook his head and walked away with shoulders hunched. Within one day I had several mothers complaining about Joe's indiscretion. Ignorance was bliss. They accepted my apologies and explanations. Pussy in England was short for pussy cat – kitten!

Joe's occasional lack of social graces caused a problem when we were enjoying a beer at Diego"s Bar and Grill near the ocean in Pacific Beach. In a crowded outside bar area, Joe farted and started to laugh. A man sitting next to us with his wife angrily turned to John and demanded,

"How dare you fart in front of my wife." Calmly Joe replied,

"I didn't realize it was her turn." Great response. Fortunately, the man laughed and all was well.

Joe soon blended in with the Mission Bay players and parents, and the club was running well and gaining a reputation in the San Diego soccer community

1983 MBSC Tour to England – Not One Boring Day

I had asked Hank if he thought the parents would support the idea of me taking a group of our players to England on a soccer tour. Hank was totally enthusiastic and relished the idea of joining me as a Tour Leader to "Jolly Old England."

A favorite, typical English joke that I told was to highlight one of the differences in the two countries: "A pair of male Siamese Twins were sitting at the bar at LAX Airport. One asked the bartender for two double whiskeys.

"We are on our way to England," the Siamese twin explained.

"I love England," said the bartender enthusiastically.

"We hate it!" said both Siamese twins. Somewhat surprised, the bartender tried again.

"I love the historic buildings, great pubs, and their sense of humor." Replied one brother,

"England sucks!" Exasperated, the bartender demanded,

"Then why the hell are you both going?!" One twin replied,

"Because it's the only place my brother can drive a car!!!"""

The response from the Mission Bay parents was incredibly positive. We had enough players for two teams – U/12 and U/18 - to go on the tour. As I write this book in 2009, I now look back on the 14 tours to England since this initial venture.

My best friend in England, Mike, was a former school teaching colleague who also worked part time several evenings a week at a youth center in my old neighborhood, Moston in North Manchester. He enthusiastically offered to get the boys accommodated for free in the youth center. I cared for Mike as a good friend, despite the fact that he was already a long way down the path to alcoholism. He was a lovable young man with a heart of gold. I had been best man at his wedding, and watched with sadness as his marriage quickly dissolved, ending in divorce. My departure to live in the USA had been a huge blow to Mike who regularly came with me at night to my show business gigs.

We arrived safe and sound at Moston Youth Center, and the 27 American boys began to unpack next to their mattresses. The sleeping arrangements were a bit primitive, but everybody was too excited to care. Hank was like a child in a candy store. Immediately, my players went downstairs and joined in the activities of the youth club; table tennis, indoor soccer, cricket, and other games. Mike had found us the perfect base for our Tour.

The next day with Hank and me driving two minibuses, we headed off to visit the most famous soccer stadium in the world – Manchester United's home field – Old Trafford! It was a magical experience to visit the changing rooms, see the trophy exhibits, sit in the dug-out where the players and manager/coaches did on game days. After the tour, it was a short journey of a few hundred yards across Salford Bridge, to the school where I had taught for six years before emigrating. I had arranged for both my teams to play games against two Ordsall High School teams.

Ordsall is an extremely tough inner-city area just outside of Manchester City Center. The school was opposite the Salford Dock Gates – a million miles from San Diego, the Pacific Ocean, and glistening sandy beaches.

When we arrived in our mini-buses, we were surrounded by a throng of ill-disciplined, noisy, excited Ordsall schoolchildren. With their noses pressed against the mini-bus windows, I heard several amusing comments, "Look, they're Americans," "Don't they dress weird," "We'll kick the shit out of them when the games begin." "They look like woofters (effeminate) with their long shorts and long blond hair."

Welcome to Ordsall, one of Britain's most deprived, dangerous area. As I stepped from the mini-bus, several of the older students recognized me as their former teacher. "Shit! it's Illingworth" (boy),

"Sir looks cute with his suntan," (girl – fortunately),

"I thought we'd seen the last of that bastard years ago!" (numerous kids)

Yes, a royal welcome back! My former colleague, Steve, who was the Head of Physical Education for many years, slapped a couple of the foul-mouths across the head and welcomed me with a firm hand shake. "Welcome back to paradise!" he mocked. The school looked even more dismal than I remembered it on my departure two years earlier. Many of the surrounding houses were in various states of demolition, and the streets were filthy and full of trash. Nevertheless, I felt strangely warm and at home, after two years away, making a new life in America.

The two games were almost a clash of two different cultures. The tough, street-smart English boys were diving into tackles, shouting, swearing, and ill-disciplined. My American players remained organized and made use of their superior fitness. When I first coached against American soccer players in 1980 at the Dallas Cup, I remembered my shock at their skill and athleticism. This day I could see the surprise, inexorably spreading through the Ordsall team. They had expected an easy game, and as the minutes passed, their lack of fitness and regular training began to take its toll. We won both games, and there was a large group of defeated, embarrassed English boys who finally staggered away from the school fields.

My boys were in high spirits as we headed back to our accommodations at Moston youth center. Our joy was short-lived when we entered the room where the mattresses and our clothes and suitcases were stored. Clothes were scattered all over the room, suitcases were open, and much of our boys" valuables had been stolen. Even more vital, was the theft of the passports.

When my mate, Mike, arrived, his embarrassment was palpable. When I had grown up in the Moston area, it had been a lower working-class area. I was unaware that nowadays it had changed into a crime ridden ghetto. Mike brought the youth club director and we explained what had happened. Slowly shaking his head, he muttered, "Scum-bags. Why do I waste my time?" Apologizing profusely, Phil confidently promised to deal with the problem and strode away.

The next day the passports were returned "mysteriously," but the money and clothes were gone. The next night, one of the Moston boys arrived at the youth club wearing one of the stolen shirts with San Diego Chargers written on the front - not the brightest move considering the circumstances. Phil took the boy aside and questioned him. Eventually most of the stolen items were returned. It was an amazing experience for my boys from laid back Mission Bay, San Diego.

The next night, I took the U/18 team to play my old Salford All Star team who been one of England's best U/14 teams four years earlier. To strengthen my team, I was going to play (I can hear sarcastic comments from friends already) and my best friend and former coaching partner, Tony Moore, would guest play also.

The game was played at a fast pace with great skill and

in good spirit. I was delighted to meet my former players and honored by their warm welcomes. This time, England triumphed. The Salford young men knew too much, and despite great performances from my team, we lost 4 – 2.

Straight across from the field was the local pub, The Racecourse. Both teams showered, changed, and walked across the street for the after game party. It was fascinating to watch the reticence of these 18 year old American young men to go to the bar and order a beer. All the English guys had been going in pubs for a long time even though the legal drinking age is 18. I had received the approval of the parents back in San Diego to allow their sons to visit pubs and drink "moderately."

Eventually my players started to settle in and relax, mixing well with their English counterparts. Finally it was time to leave, as I had arranged for my players to visit a popular night club in downtown Manchester. As we left the Pub, I shook hands with the landlord, Doug, who I had known for many years. I counted all my players as we walked onto the car park and we departed for downtown Manchester. With all our farewells over, we drove the mini-buses to a superb night club, Fagins, owned by an old friend of mine, John Bagnall. As I escorted the players into the club, I decided to do another head count. We were missing a player! I checked who it was and realized we were missing Robert. I asked the rest of the group if they had any idea what had happened to him, since I had counted everybody back at the pub car park. One of the boys said that Robert had dashed back into the pub to use the restroom. I phoned the Racecourse pub and spoke to my friend, the landlord.

"Yes, he is here Jeff. No worries."

I offered to drive back and pick him up. Robert came on the phone and begged me to let him stay there, socializing with the locals. The landlord offered to let him stay and give him breakfast before we would pick him up the next morning.

"No problem, Jeff. He is with my two sons in the bar. My wife and I will take care of him."

The next morning I picked up a tired-looking, but very happy 18 year old who had "Died and gone to heaven – locked overnight in a great English Pub!"

The next few days went well, visiting the Beatles museum in Liverpool and the beautiful, ancient Roman town of Chester.

We set off for our journey to England's capital city, London, arriving at our accommodations, Royal Holloway College, near Windsor Castle. This was the first All-Female College in the World. The campus was a series of majestic old buildings, beautiful surroundings, and a breathtaking chapel.

The next day I took the two teams on a tour of Windsor Castle, one of Queen Elizabeth's royal homes. As the tour guide took us around the magnificent castle, I began to tire of a wealthy, elderly American couple in our group. As we viewed the stately dining room, the elderly lady, obviously from New York, said to her husband, "Honey, that dining room set would look so good in our house in the Hamptons!" Passing under an enormous, glittering chandelier, she said, "Oh my! That chandelier would be perfect for our place in Florida, darling!" Viewing a painting on the wall of a great artist, she shrilled, "Oh my – on the wall of our penthouse in Manhattan ...." At that moment a jet plane from nearby Heathrow Airport roared overhead. Never one to miss making her presence felt, the elderly New York lady quipped, "The English are so quaint! Imagine building a castle on a flight path!!" Hearing this incredibly inane remark from this boorish lady, I spun around to educate her. Obviously embarrassed, her husband, red-faced, held up his hand and said,

"I know. I know. Please excuse us," as he led his confused wife away to explain her consummate faux pas.

The next day we toured London on foot. The Tower of London enthralled my players as they heard tales of beheadings and executions. Buckingham Palace and an eventful visit followed to the store for the rich – Harrods. We all enjoyed the fantastic toy department, and before we knew it, we were putting on a karaoke show for many of the surprised customers. Most Harrods shoppers tend to be older, wealthy, conservative types. Here was my group of fun-loving, young Southern Californians giving a lively, impromptu performance of Beach Boys songs.

Driving out of London in heavy traffic, I had to stop to ask for directions to our college accommodations which were 20 miles outside of London. Hank then attempted to equal the foolishness of the American lady at Windsor Castle.

"I thought you grew up in England. You can't have forgotten your way around in a couple of years," Hank whined.

"Hank, I grew up in Manchester – 200 miles away. London is one of the world's most difficult cities to find your way around. Hank, you grew up in San Diego. Do you know your way around Chicago?" The argument was lost on him as he shook his head, confused.

The next day we headed to the airport for our return to San Diego. The group of boys had enjoyed one final night of excitement, thanks to Hank"s incredible pranks. Near to where we were staying was a very ancient cemetery, which Hank had told the boys was haunted. When it was dark, he drove the younger boys to the cemetery. The older boys feigned indifference and begged out of the trip.

Meanwhile, they secretly headed to the cemetery carrying white sheets and ghost masks that Hank had provided. As Hank slowly led our younger boys around the dark, eerie cemetery, "ghosts" started to appear from behind distant graves and disappear into the night again. The young guys were terrified and pandemonium broke out similar (to Hank's occasional soccer coaching sessions). Honestly, Hank played the scene up to maximum, and it was a superb final night to a thrilling soccer tour.

As we took off from Heathrow heading home, I was surprised to see one of the airline stewardesses heading sternly toward me.

"You will have to take control of your group. They are upsetting other passengers by making too much noise," she ordered. That was strange. I was sitting only a couple of rows back and hadn't heard any noise whatsoever. I left my seat and slowly walked forward, listening for a cacophony of noise. Nothing! The boys were all sitting in their seats behaving fine. Across the aisle was a middle-aged couple with "sleeping masks" on their foreheads.

"Are you in charge of this group?" asked the man angrily. I was none too pleased by his manner and thought both of them looked ridiculous with sleeping masks at 11:00 AM in the morning.

"I certainly am. What is your problem, other than the obvious one that you don't like children," I replied sarcastically.

"Who do you think you are talking to?" he asked menacingly.

"You. Who else?" I replied. As he tried to jump up from the seat, I grabbed him firmly with one hand.

"If you want to sleep at lunchtime on a packed flight in coach class, that's your problem, not mine."

The flight attendants were in panic. One of the pilots

came rushing back, threatening to turn the plane around. Order was restored when they wisely moved the couple to another part of the planc. Fourteen hours later, we arrived safely in San Diego without further incident.

Disturbingly, two years later a similar incident occurred. I have done some research since and the problem is simple. Many older people don't like to be surrounded by a large group of children on a long flight.

MBSC 1983 – 1985 – David v Goliath

Heading into my third year at MBSC, I had a great assistant, Coach Joe, a successful England tour behind me, and the original 5 weak teams had now increased to 12, with many of them high quality. Several of our teams were now highly competitive and a real sense of competition was developing between us and our neighbors, the elite La Jolla Nomads Club. This was specifically true in the younger ages – U/8 to U/12 boys. Interestingly enough, neither the Nomads nor we had any girl's teams. So at this stage, my coaching commitments and focus was on boys only. Another factor was the high percentage of highly skilled Hispanic players from South San Diego playing for the Nomads whereas we had none.

Coach Joe had found a part time job as an assistant waiter at a top class local Italian restaurant, Casino Valadier. The problem was that Joe had no experience either working or dining in top restaurants! Problems began at the outset. The black jacket provided for him was three sizes too large. He couldn't understand the accents of the Italian waiters. He never looked smart or possessed elegance at the best of times. He was a "fish out of water." His great sense of humor was lost on his Italian co-workers. "What is the smallest book in the world? The book of Italian war heroes!" Not amused. "Why are Italians able to get suntanned on the inside part of their forearms? Because they are always walking with their hands on their heads during the two World Wars!"

After only a couple of weeks at Casino Valadier, the owner approached Joe. "Joe, you have never worked in a top restaurant before, but I like you." Two more incidents were to quickly bring the whole debacle to an end.

One evening, a waiter told Joe to clear the plates off

Table 7. Joe saw that the plates were not yet empty and waited. Rushing past, the waiter twice told John again to clear Table 7. Finally in exasperation, Joe pointed out that there was still food on the plates. Even more exasperated, the waiter screamed at him that the "food on the plate" were the shells of the oysters that the diners had finished 15 minutes earlier. The end arrived mercifully for Joe when he efficiently cleared the table of all plates, knives, forks, cups, saucers, and napkins. The eight dining customers sat quietly staring at a completely empty table as he proudly headed to the kitchen bearing his load of used dinner utensils. Unfortunately passing him going the other way was the Head Waiter, Salvatore, carrying eight entrees toward the table Joe had just cleared! As John disappeared into the kitchen, Salvatore arrived at the "barren" table. As the diners and waiter stared blankly at each other, Joe reappeared. Salvatore looked at him and moved his head in the direction of the table. Joe was equally confused until he noticed the eight plates of steaming food balanced on the waiter's shoulder. Slowly the realization dawned on Joe. The meals were for the people sitting at the table he had cleared. Defensively he responded weakly, "I thought they had finished. They have had three courses already." Unfortunately, they were paying for five courses! By the time the table was reset and the meals were reheated, Joe had already returned his jacket as requested and he was out of the restaurant. Arriving at my apartment, he gladly accepted a beer and committed himself to soccer coaching, knowing his restaurant career was over.

The next 12months, Chugger, TK, Darren, my "franchise players," scored goals, led their teams by example, and we continued to progress as a club. However, success brings its own problems. A couple of mothers began muttering that Chugger was a ball hog. "If only he would pass it more, we would score more goals as a team!" I totally disagreed, and without any subtlety told them they were wrong and probably jealous. Tact had never been my strength, and it was to prove a problem then and in the years to come.

TK was also scoring goals, and I was soon to become a close friend of his father, Bob, who to this day is still one of my very best friends and a neighbor in Del Mar. "Never judge a book by its cover" could describe my first impression of Bob. He was dressed in casual beach wear, had a nonchalant attitude, and made no attempt to schmooze anybody. If I had to guess his profession, I would have guessed construction or factory work. We had a simple, straight-forward relationship. He respected and supported my coaching of his son, and I appreciated his direct, open behavior and attitude. It was by pure chance I was to discover that Bob was in fact a highly successful stock-broker of national repute. He managed a successful brokerage firm in the wealthy town of La Jolla. He also had an impressive list of successful clients of his own. During out of town tournaments, we discovered we had many mutual interests. Bob played keyboards in a band and was fascinated to hear about my long career in show business in England as a stand-up comedian.

Chugger"s parents, Chuck and Ginger, also became close friends of my wife and me. We spent Christmas Eve at their church and had Christmas lunch at their home. Chuck and Ginger allowed us to feel a part of a family, which meant so much to us as our family was 6,000 miles away. Having parents of great players, as close friends, makes life easier in one way. At least the other parents in the team couldn't complain that I was only playing TK and Chugger because of my friendship with their parents.

Nevertheless, I began to hear whispers of "Jeff prefers to socialize only with the parents of the 'star' players." While teaching in England in high schools, I had never run into teacher/parent socializing problems because I taught in lower income areas and I lived many miles away. This USA pro-soccer coach/parent relationship was unchartered territory as "competitive" soccer in 1981 was in its infancy.

When summer rolled around after three seasons at MBSC, I took Joe with me to help with the camps in Bakersfield. It was great having him along with his great humor, excellent teaching skills, and personality that all kids and parents loved. At the end of the day late in the week, a father approached me and introduced himself as the parent of a nice young boy in Joe's group. He explained that they lived in Mammoth Lakes but the father was working a contract in Bakersfield. He had his son with him for the week and was grateful to have him at my camp enjoying himself. I explained that I was only in Bakersfield to direct my camps – my home was in San Diego. The father then explained that he was on the board of the local soccer organization in Mammoth Lakes. He felt strongly that he could arrange for me to run a couple of soccer camps in his town. Another great business opportunity had appeared. Little did I know what a beautiful location I was being offered.

True to his word, he called me that weekend and invited me to run a soccer camp in Mammoth Lakes at the end of that summer. He educated me that their soccer season only lasted 4 _ months due to weather conditions. The League was totally recreational and having an "English pro-coach" visit their town/village had created a stir of excitement.

For me, I was adjusting to my increasing reputation as

a successful pro-coach running Camps in San Diego, Bakersfield, and now Mammoth Lakes. Less than four years earlier, I was coaching and running school teams for free as part of my school teaching job in the Manchester area of England.

When the end of summer arrived, Joe and I make the long seven hour drive to Mammoth Lakes. Despite hearing of Mammoth Lake's reputation for beauty, I was stunned as we headed out of the town of Bishop, climbing steeply up the Mountain. Famous as a world class ski resort, Mammoth has an equal appeal when the snow has cleared - crystal clear lakes, soaring trees, pure blue skies and fresh, fresh air.

From the beauty of Ski Beach in San Diego, training my Mission Bay players, through the torrid heat of the Bakersfield camps, to the majesty of this tiny soccer field deep in the heart of the forest of Mammoth Lakes. Soccer camps were, and still are, the rewarding, joyful, lucrative, "icing on the cake" for a pro youth soccer coach. The children have lots of fun while receiving experience by playing many hours of soccer games and drills. For the coaches, there are relatively few parent complaints and no need to worry about playing time, what positions children play, or winning games.

Soccer in Mammoth Lakes was soccer in its purest form, with most of the children skilled skiers but novice soccer players, great attitudes, and huge enthusiasm. The week passed quickly with Joe and me getting to meet many of the locals through our sponsors, the O'Sullivan family.

As we departed from their home very early Saturday morning, I looked across the street to see a huge bear on all fours, sitting outside the front door of the neighbor's house opposite us. I quickly signally to Joe, I then saw the bear look across at us and stand fearsomely on two huge legs. Unsure whether to return to the house or dive into the car, we waited hopefully to see what the bear would do. Finally, the bear dropped onto all fours, and with surprising speed, bounded off down the street. My car at the time was a two-seater sports car with a soft top. Had the bear raced toward us, I realized later that jumping into the "safety" of the car would have been a fatal mistake. Several years later, one of my coaches left food in his Mercedes sedan and a bear tore off the door to get at the food.

As we drove down the mountain early that morning we felt joyfully alive and peaceful, truly grateful for a summer of successful, financially rewarding camps and energized by the thought of my upcoming fourth season as Coaching Director of Mission Bay Soccer Club. Whenever everything seems absolutely perfect in youth soccer, storm clouds are often gathering somewhat out of sight. Joe and I enjoyed our return journey with the roof down on my car, the wind whipping through our (my!) hair (remember Joe is "hair impaired").

The fourth season began well with both of us working hard and enjoying our coaching sessions with our 16 teams in our, once again expanded Club. After practice, one of our parents approached me about a coaching opportunity at one of the large, local San Diego universities. They were looking to create a Girls NCAA Soccer program, and the father was a senior member of the Faculty. Would I be interested in the coaching opportunity? It was an intriguing offer and certainly had great potential over the forthcoming years for whoever took on the challenge. With my increasing number of summer soccer camps and steadily expanding number of Mission Bay teams, I reluctantly decided that the University opportunity would need too much of my time, especially during the summer months. However, Joe, no longer involved in the restaurant business, had many free hours available. One problem was that he had no legal work permit! In the early 1980's, before the 9/11 catastrophe, there was far less scrutiny of people's legal work status. We finally set up a deal where Joe would be the actual coach and I would be the coach of record. I would be paid by the University and I would then give the money to Joe. Working with a highly intelligent group of 18 and 19 year old young Southern California girls was beyond his wildest dreams. He threw himself into the challenge of building a Girls Collegiate program from the ground up. In his inimitable, humorous manner he would ask, "Where in the world can you get paid great money for telling beautiful young ladies to "Show me your cleats?!""

Both Joe and I had taught in high schools in the Northern English city of Salford; inner city children from tough, often broken homes, persistent absence from schools, fights, lack of parent support and teaching apathy. Now we were both totally immersed in youth soccer and university/college programs with talented, motivated youngsters in sunny Southern California. I was delighted to have helped him once again to obtain another coaching opportunity and boost his income.

Both of us admired the hard work Hank put into organizing MBSC and the Mission Bay Classic Tournament. Neither of us admired his coaching of any of the teams, nor did we have a close social relationship together. Nevertheless, we were both extremely grateful to him for the huge opportunities he had given us both. On occasion, Hank's lack of good financial management would mean a problem with payment of our wages. On one occasion, he said he didn't have enough to pay Joe. I told him neither of us would work unless we were both paid. From somewhere, the money was found and we continued on. Hank was involved for the fun/social aspect, enjoying spending time with all the boys. Every summer he would take a group on a month long trip across America in his mini-bus. One year he took the group to Minnesota where we had a soccer connection with a club that had played in the MB Classic Tournament.

"Whenever It Is Too Good To Be True"

During our fourth season, everything was going well at the Club, and my wife, Pauline, now had a full time teaching job. I reflected on my first year in San Diego when I had an opportunity to join a sports clothing company struggling to get into the soccer business. I had been offered an interview at their head office and was pretty much guaranteed the job, which would have forced me to relocate to San Jose, in Northern California. On Sunday afternoon, the day before I was due to fly North for the interview, I looked out of the window of our apartment on Mission Bay to see sunbathers on the beach, boats sailing by, joggers on the Boardwalk, and Sea World in the distance. I realized that there was no way I wanted to give this up to relocate to San Jose. We had left England for one reason only – to live in San Diego. Despite losing me as a potential District Manager for Soccer Equipment Sales Development, Nike seems to have managed to cope!!!

Now four years later, I was enjoying my part time school teaching job and totally immersed in running MBSC. Joe and I ran five miles daily on the oceanfront and played golf on Fridays at beautiful Torrey Pines Golf Course.

Hank, Joe and I traveled to Los Angeles for a soccer tournament,. On Saturday night after the game, Hank was only too happy to stay at the hotel with the players. Joe and I headed out for relaxation and a meal, arriving back at the hotel about 1:00 AM. Surprisingly, Hank was on the balcony and asked to speak to me. Joe left and went to his room. Entering Hank's hotel room, I sensed tension in the air and was intrigued by his rather formal manner.

His first words were to tear my world apart. "What would you say if I were to ask you to resign?" I was stunned and stared directly into his face, disbelieving what I had just heard. Over the past four years, I had never taken Hank too seriously, and on occasion, probably treated him with scant regard. Suddenly I was looking into the eyes of the one man who could destroy my wonderful, new found life in America. Trying to bluff my way out of my panic, I replied,

"You have never been able to tell any good jokes, Hank."

"No," he said coldly. "You are the one who makes everybody laugh and gets all the praise and the attention."

Now I knew there was a serious problem. Our roles in the Club were very clear, yet totally without any contracts or agreed structure. He had started MBSC and worked hard to organize its day to day running. Many of the original parents appreciated Hank's "babysitting service" and summer trips with their sons. Many of the newer parents, like TK's dad, Bob, and Chugger's parents were committed to serious soccer and had little respect for Hank's laissez-faire approach.

For the first time in our relationship, we faced each other as new, serious adversaries. Calmly I asked, "Where and why has this situation arisen? The Club is doing great and the players and parents are happy." Seemingly unable to clarify his questions, he suggested I think about his question and opened his door, invited me to leave.

When I arrived back at the hotel room, I was sharing with Joe. I was in a state of shock. When I looked at him, I realized immediately that he had some idea of what was going on. "What did he say to you, Jeff?" Joe asked. I replied, "He asked me to resign," I blurted out pathetically. Only one hour earlier, we had been singing and dancing.

Now I was under threat of losing my job – a job I had

created, developed, and believed in. I also felt uneasy that Joe had known something was going on and had not fore-warned me.

Over the next 25 years, this would not be the last time I was to discover that support and trust from friends and colleagues in youth soccer coaching cannot be taken for granted.

The next day, the atmosphere during the games was tense and uncomfortable with me mistrustful of both Joe and Hank. I spoke to TK's dad, Bob, who was by now a very close friend of mine.

"He's crazy if he thinks he can get rid of you. We are not here for Hank's pizza parties and summer trips. We are here because of you and your great soccer program." Bob's words gave me some comfort, but driving back to San Diego, I tried to envision life in San Diego without coaching soccer at MBSC. I also spoke to Chugger's parents, Chuck and Ginger, who had also become friends with Joe. They were very supportive of me and again had little respect for Hank as a role model or soccer expert.

Over the next few weeks, the situation was confused and unpleasant with pro-Jeff groups appearing, and surprising to me, anti-Jeff parents stepping forward to support Hank. It was also becoming apparent that Joe's position was extremely untenable. He owed me a great deal and had been practically a member of our family with Pauline and me welcoming him into our home. Both his job at MBSC and the University were his, directly because of my support. We had been friends for 16 years, since meeting as freshmen students at Didsbury College, Manchester in 1968. If I were to be forced out, he would certainly receive a promotion and increased pay and prospects.

As the crisis moved toward some form of necessary

resolution, I confronted Joe directly.

"Hank cannot run the Club without both of us. I need your support. You have been like a family member, and unless you know of something that I have done wrong in the Club, why should I resign?" I was looking for unequivocal support from my old friend and waited tensely for Joe's response.

"Jeff, you have done a great job at MBSC, and it would not be where it is without you." I dreaded what else might be about to come.

"Unfortunately, Jeff, you have made enemies along the way. Several mothers have harbored grudges against you since you accused them of jealously of TK and Chugger. Other parents don't like your strong discipline, which is so different from Hank's original club atmosphere. Hank feels you have taken over the club and he is 'just a dogsbody.'"

The storm clouds were not going away. In fact, they were darkening, and rumor and innuendo were rife throughout the Club. "As one door closes, another slams shut." How true!

Finally, Hank arranged a parents meeting to rally support for his plan to get rid of me. I was not invited. The meeting was explosive with Bob, Chuck and Ginger, and other committed soccer parents arguing for me, and other parents supporting Hank, saying it was time for a change of coaching leadership. Joe's name was mooted as my replacement. Ultimately, like President Nixon in the Watergate scandal, it was inevitable that my time was over. As Sir Anthony Hopkins (President Nixon) says in Nixon, the movie, "It's only when you are on the bottom of the valley that you realize how great the view was from the top of the mountain."

The meeting ended with a split group of parents, and

my future looked bleak at MBSC. After discussing the situation over the following few weeks, I realized that Hank was still committed to getting rid of me.

The final straw was provided by me. One of our younger teams, coached on the day by Hank, had lost 10 – 0 to the El Cajon Hotspurs on our home field! I was disgusted when I heard what a shambles the game had been - some of our players running off the field or refusing to be substituted back on. As chance would have it, the following week we were due to play them again at their field in El Cajon, 15 miles inland. I made sure that the coaching schedule for that day had me coaching that game.

I arrived early and started an intensive warm up with our boys. I had insisted that all the players arrive on time and was focused on restoring our pride. Our opponents were relaxed, and I could see lots of laughing and joking on the other side of the field. I was treating the game as a Cup Final with my adrenaline flowing. The night before the game, Friday, I had stayed home and gone to bed early. (OK, that's a lie, but you get the point!) I was pumped up!

The game began, and from the beginning, I was ecstatic to see my team competing for every ball. Gradually it dawned on the Hotspurs players that this would not be a repeat of the previous week's debacle. As the game progressed, I was disgusted with the performance of the referee. Not only was he bad, but I felt he was biased toward the Hotspurs. They scored first and smiles came back on their faces. We equalized and Game On! In the second half, the tension mounted with our team taking the lead 2 -1. Now the Hotspurs coach and parents were going crazy. I continued to drive my players forward. "Be aggressive. Challenge for the ball. TACKLE!" Several mothers on the other side screamed every time a strong challenge happened against their sons. My "cute little beach dudes" were beating up on the "tough Valley boys." Out of nowhere, the referee awarded a penalty against us for a strong but legal challenge in our penalty box. I went "ballistic," accusing him of cheating and being intimidated by their parents. I was out of control and deserved to be sent off – I WAS! Red carded, I slouched to the car park like a churlish schoolboy. They scored from the penalty and we hung on at 2-2 until the final whistle. It was a fantastic turn around in a week from 10-0 to 2-2, marred only by my embarrassing behavior.

Obviously the referee reported the red card to the Presidio League, and I faced a severe punishment. My phone rang several days later and it was a member of the Presidio League. Speaking "off the record," he informed me that Hank had secretly contacted the Presidio League about my red card. He had asked them to give me the "maximum punishment available" so he could get me out of his Club and the League. Hearing this, impetuously (as usual), I phoned Hank telling him what I had just heard. He made a half-hearted attempt to deny it. "Hank, you want me to resign. You got it. I resign as of now! Show me how well Mission Bay Soccer Club runs with you as the driving force!"

It was done. Pauline stared at me. "Do you know what you have just done?" she stammered. At the moment, I felt a sense of relief and vindication. The "hangover" would begin the next day.

Next morning, my phone never stopped ringing with parents either angry, shocked, or offering their support. Several of the top players' parents indicated that they would move their sons to play for me at another Club if I found a new coaching position. The problem was there were no paid pro-soccer coaching positions existing at any youth soccer clubs other than the La Jolla Nomads. It was over, and for days when 3:30 rolled around, I felt this huge sense of loss and emptiness. Only a mile away from my apartment on the beach, MBSC youngsters were training – without me there. Occasionally I would drive by, surreptitiously, like a stalker, newly divorced from his wife!

A few weeks later I heard that Hank had hired a new coach to replace me. He was a well known German soccer player who played for the famous local Indoor Pro team, The San Diego Sockers. Strange bedfellows, with Coach Joe as English as fish and chips and Coach G as German as sauerkraut.

Obviously my relationship with Joe had soured and it led to a disagreement between my wife, Pauline, and Chugger's mom, Ginger. Usually the best of friends, my wife told Ginger how disgusted she was that Joe had not backed me to the hilt. Defending Joe, Ginger pointed out what a difficult position he had been forced into. Pauline asked Ginger if she would be magnanimous if it were her husband who had lost his job, especially when his best friend stayed on working for the Bad Guy.

Fortunately, in the long run, this emotional situation did not ruin the deep friendship between me, Pauline, and Chuck and Ginger. I was the one who was to do that, on my own, sadly!

Reprieved – Just in Time – 1987
The Hotspurs 1985-1987

For several weeks after my unpleasant departure from MBSC, I drifted through my school job, ran on the Boardwalk and swam at Jack La Laines. Seemingly an idyllic existence, but in fact it I was drifting, pondering going back to England and resuming my old life in P.E. teaching and show business.

I also felt uncomfortable in the local Mission Bay community, often bumping into parents from MBSC. Some were friendly and sympathetic, others lukewarm, and some pointedly ignored me.

"How Are The Mighty Fallen!" One mother came up to me with a smile on her face in Diego's Mexican Restaurant and asked sarcastically, "How are you doing Coach? My son is doing great since you were fired. He plays more now."

England began to look better and better. One Sunday evening, my wife and I walked along the bay, and sensing my melancholy mood, she asked what was going on.

"Sorry, Pauline but I feel lost and lonely. I am used to working two jobs, day and night. Without my soccer coaching, I feel useless. I wonder whether we should go back to live in England." We walked back to our apartment in silence.

I noticed the telephone message light flashing and switched it on. It was the President of the El Cajon Hotspurs Soccer Club asking me to call him immediately. Intrigued, I called immediately and was stunned to receive an offer to be their first ever Professional Director of Coaching. Back from the brink!

A few days later after meeting the Board of the Hotspurs Club, I accepted the job gratefully. It was a large

Club, established much longer than Mission Bay S.C. and run by a Board – not one man. I would not coach any teams of my own, but would oversee, help, and guide the many volunteer coaches in the Club. It was somehow ironic that the very Club that inadvertently led to my demise from MBSC had now rescued me.

Once the job was confirmed, I contacted several of my former parents of my top players. TK, Chugger, Jim Wong, and Todd Emblem were four great players whose parents all were happy to follow me and join the Hotspurs Club, despite the forty minute each way round trip from the beach inland to El Cajon. Losing these great players was a huge blow to the infrastructure of my former Club.

Over the next two years while I was directing the Hotspurs Club, I followed closely the situation at MBSC. Joe was acutely unhappy working with his German counterpart, and our relationship started to heal. He gave me regular reports on the chaos and disorder within my old club. Although having a sense of satisfaction, I disliked seeing something I had helped build begin to crumble. It would not be the first time, or the last, I would experience this bittersweet scenario.

Mission Bay Soccer Club was inexorably reverting back, it seemed clear, to being a "happy go lucky" soccer club, lacking real purpose or competitive desire. Several more dedicated players began to drift away to other clubs.

I settled in to my new job, accepting the 34 mile round trip daily as worthwhile and necessary, grateful to have gained re-employment in a career that still didn't really exist. Chugger arrived to play in a superb under 14 team coached and managed by a great man, Rex Burnett. Rex was the father of one of the players, his son Brett. Although without any soccer background or playing experience, Rex controlled and directed the team with great skill. He was a successful businessman, and the boys showed their respect to the man they only ever called "Mr. Burnett." The team was a group of local boys who had been together for many years. The goalkeeper was superb, and up front, Scott Hargrove was a forward of national level. Adding Chugger to this group was a win/win situation. The team improved and Chugger was finally surrounded by players of similar quality.

Playing a game in nearby Ramona, Rex's team thrashed a team 10-3 whilst I watched the game thinking I was seeing double. I was! Ramona had a set of twins who were great players and gave us a great deal of trouble. They were obviously playing on that team because they had their mates there. After the game, I introduced myself to their parents and invited them to come and practice with us. Derek and Darren Drago joined our team and made us even stronger.

I enjoyed working with Rex and was delighted to have Chugger and his parents around me again. TK had also been fortunate to join a top class Hotspurs team who had been our mortal enemy when we were at MBSC. The two guys who coached the team, Jim and Howie, had been instrumental in getting me hired at the Hotspurs. They were totally dedicated to their boys, and were stunned to be able to add TK to their team. Unlike Rex, however, they did not have the firm control and discipline of their players, and even more so, the parents. They were both simply too nice, and without a doubt, there was some jealousy and resentment toward TK. Bob was happy to have shown his support for me, and as a great athlete himself, enjoyed seeing TK playing at the highest level.

The summer before leaving MBSC, I had taken a second group to England, including a great boy called Kurt Yokes who had joined Mission Bay as an inexperienced player. In short time he picked up the game and quickly became a strong, skilled player. His personality was delightful and sunny. Always smiling, he was immediately accepted by his teammates and their parents.

Kurt Yokes – In Memoriam

Kurt was another TK with long, blond hair, suntanned, big smile, and lovable personality. His dad, Bob, was an older parent who adored Kurt and was at every practice and every game. Bob owned his own successful flower shop in Pacific Beach, allowing him free time to be with his son. On our England Tour, I housed Kurt in Manchester at the home of my best mate, Tony Moore, and his wife, Christine. They had three great boys of their own and fell in love with Kurt Yokes. When we returned to the USA, Bob sent the Moore Family a beautiful white, leather bound bible with a sincere thank you message on the inside front cover. Kurt had gone off to play for the La Jolla Nomads and I was sorry to lose touch with him and his father, Bob.

At the end of my first year at the Hotspurs, I took a group of their players to England, including Chugger, for a second time. He had actually stayed on previously and lived with the Moore family for several months. TK was to do the same, breaking the hearts of many young English girls who fell in love with his California good looks and cute American accent. Yes! Americans do have an accent! In fact, many accents.

Returning to the USA with a happy group after a successful tour, I was in high spirits. During the trip, Chugger had been involved in a hilarious incident. In London, we had gone to lunch in a local fish and chip shop. The weather was unusually hot – over 80 degrees in a country where air conditioning in the mid-1980s didn't exist, and refrigerators were still a luxury. Chugger stood at the counter and ordered a Coke. The shop assistant leaned in the front window and took a Coke can off the shelf and gave it to Chugger. Having been on the shelf for hours with the sun shining on it, the can was not only not chilled, it was bloody hot. Barely able to hold the can, Chugger juggled it from hand to hand, looking at it as though it was an object from outer space. I couldn't help myself. "What's wrong Chugger?" I asked, tongue in cheek. He couldn't put into words the fact that the Coke can was not chilled and was totally undrinkable. A cultural difference for sure!

Arriving at San Diego Airport, I met my wife, Pauline, with a smile on my face, happy to be home. The news she gave me was too incredibly sad to be true. Kurt Yokes had been murdered two days before by the owner of a Chinese Restaurant in Pacific Beach – a restaurant we used regularly. There had been some sort of traffic altercation between the restaurant owner and Kurt and his two friends. The owner had followed their car up Soledad Mountain Road, and as the three teenagers walked away from their car, tragically, inexplicably, he had opened his car window and shot Kurt with a gun. Immediately my thoughts went to Kurt's dad. I rarely saw his mother, but he had several siblings and it was a super family.

The funeral was a nightmare with dozens of people crying, including me, and his father in a seemingly catatonic state. It was, and still is, to me the worst loss of a human life I have ever experienced. I was beginning to realize how far reaching the effects soccer coaching had on ME. Different from teaching in a school, my new coaching career brought me close to the players, and by its very nature, close to their families.

Before the shock of Kurt's death could begin to heal, I was contacted by an attorney representing the Yokes family. At the murder trial, the restaurant owner had received a meager five year sentence in jail. Next there was to be a Civil Trial against the man's insurance company. I gave a deposition and was then asked to attend Court to give evidence.

During this time, my wife and I had decided after sixteen years together to try to have a family. Helping me to decide was my admiration and respect for the father/son relationship I had for Bob Yokes and Kurt and Bob Inbody and his son, TK.

When the attorney representing the insurance company asked me why or how Bob and Kurt's relationship was different from any other father/son relationship, he didn't like my answer. "In 14 years of teaching and coaching both here and in England, Bob and Kurt's relationship was the most heartwarming father/son relationship I have ever had the pleasure to witness. It was their example to me that convinced me to try and have a child of my own after sixteen years with my wife."

The response seemed to grab the attention of the attorney and the Court. The case was settled that day. However, no amount of money could ever take away the profound sense of loss we all felt at losing such a wonderful young man. His father seemed to become reclusive, and I have never seen him in twenty years. I did have the pleasure of meeting one of his brothers a few ago.

The bible sent to England still proudly sits on the small table outside the bedroom of my friend"s bedroom in memory of their former house guest.

As my second year as Director of Coaching began, the Hotspurs Club was doing well and we had several state champion teams to be proud of. Chugger's team had beaten the La Jolla Nomads, much to the surprise of their Pro Head Coach, Derek Armstrong in the semi-final. Despite the success, I missed coaching my own teams and the long journey out to El Cajon was beginning to wear on me.

One evening at home, I received a call from a stranger who was staying at Oakwood Garden Apartments in Pacific Beach. Like me four years ago, this Englishman was new in the country and looking to get some type of work. He was married to an American lady and had been a Pro First Divisional soccer player in England. Could I give him any assistance? I agreed to meet him the next morning, Saturday, outside his apartment building and take him with me to Los Angeles for a big soccer tournament.

Next morning, Saturday, in my car with the roof down outside my former home, Oakwood Apartments, I waited for him to appear. Suddenly a dirty, disheveled guy leaned into my car. Oh no! I couldn't possibly drive this street bum with me all the way to Los Angles. "Nice car man. Can you spare a couple of dollars?" Thank God, this was not my fellow countryman!

A minute later, a blond, handsome, athletic guy ran down the steps of the building. "Hi, I"m Colin. Thanks for taking the trouble to do this. Great Car!" "No problem. Jump in. This will be a long day, but I will try to give you as much information as I can. We enjoyed each other's company and had a busy few days going from one Hotspurs game to another. He had been a successful Pro in England, at a far higher level than I had ever played. He was strikingly handsome with a great smile and sense of humor.

The next week, I met Colin's American wife, who not surprisingly was stunningly attractive. With Joe no longer a major friend, he became an ideal replacement with both of us running on the beach, playing tennis, and having swimming competitions.

Chugger's Hotspurs team were State Champions, and we were preparing for the Regional Finals to be held that year in Albuquerque, New Mexico. We were in fact "State Champions" of Southern California, with California being the only state to have two "State Champions."

The Regionals would include all the Western State Champions, including Alaska and Hawaii, with the winner going on to the Final Four that year in New York. As Director of Coaching, I was allowed, even encouraged, to be actively involved coaching and training the team. However, in the final analysis, it was "Mr. Burnett's" team, and I respected his position.

Over the many years of coaching in California, I have often heard the argument that the coach of a team should change every two years. Also, many consider a coach's playing experience and level to be a prerequisite. Rex Burnett never played a full game of soccer in his life. Nevertheless, as we approached the U/16 Regionals, he had managed and coached this great group of local boys for eight years. In fact, he kept the team together until they finally graduated and went off to different colleges.

Our goalkeeper, Jason, was one year younger than the rest of the team, one of the smallest players in the team, and from a single parent family. Despite these things, he was the heart of the team, making unbelievable saves, showing huge courage and agility. For the first time in many years of coaching, I fully appreciated the vital importance of a great "keeper." Several games where we deserved to lose or tie, Jason would perform the impossible, motivating his teammates to go forward and score. Besides Chugger and the speedy Scott, we had a gifted midfield general – Toby – with the Drago twins either side of him. Team spirit was high as we all boarded our flight in June to head off to New Mexico.

It was my first experience at Regionals, and I soaked up the atmosphere and experience daily, watching many great games. We were playing well, and from my scouting information, we were in with a good chance of going a long way in the Tournament. Alaska and Hawaii are beautiful places to vacation, but in 1987, their soccer programs were in the early development stages. Their State Champion teams were beat by big scores; 6-0, and 7-1 as we advanced in the Tournament. After six days, we were deservedly in the Final.

If we won the Regional Final, we would head to New York the following month to play in the National Final Four Playoffs. I had seen our opponents during the week and felt confident that we were the better team with Chugger and Scott easily capable of scoring against any opponent. I also felt that they would struggle to get the ball past our superb goalkeeper, Jason.

It was by far the biggest game I had ever coached. To reach this far, we had won a most difficult State Cup-Southern California, and we had now spent one week playing daily against the Champions of other Western U.S. States.

I studied the attitudes of our players in the build-up to the Final. I admired their low key, determined approach to the upcoming challenge.

The first half was a real battle with no real serious

threat from our opponents as we pushed to take the lead. Just before the half time whistle, there was a mix-up by the referee over a free kick. He pointed in our favor and our players started to move forward. Then the referee changed his mind and pointed the other way. The other team took advantage by taking a quick free kick and scored. I was none too pleased, but we were down 1-0.

The second half was unbelievably frustrating as we did everything but score. Heartbreakingly, the final whistle blew and it was over. The chance of a lifetime for these young men had evaporated!

To this day, that loss is the most painful in my coaching career. The other three teams to reach the Final Four were teams we had already beaten in other Tournaments. I felt absolutely sure that had we won Regionals, we would have gone on to be National Champions. My admiration for that group of young men was based not just on their great soccer talent, but a communal admiration for each other, supportive parents, and great leadership from Rex Burnett. It was not an All-Star team from everywhere, but a group of players, many of whom went to school together and lived in the same neighborhood. In 2009, I am not sure that this would be realistically possible again considering the high number of great teams.

Arriving back in San Diego in a somber mood, I was surprised to receive a call from the La Jolla Nomads offering me a coaching position on their staff. I would not be Head Coach as Derek was the Director and Brian his Assistant Director. Nevertheless, I would have my own teams. I lived close to their home field in La Jolla, and my new second career in real estate sales might benefit by working in a wealthy area like La Jolla.

After a few days weighing up both possibilities, I received an even more intriguing job offer. After running together, Colin and I arrived at my new home in North Pacific Beach. Sitting in the garden, relaxing with a glass of water, I played my phone messages.

"Hi Jeff. This is Hank. I was wondering if you would give me a call so we can arrange to meet. I would like to invite you to come back to Mission Bay Soccer Club!!!"

I was totally stunned. Although I was aware that things were not going well at my old club, I had no idea it had reached this stage. I had really mixed emotions; excitement and an adrenaline rush mixed with anger and gloating that "the wheel had come full circle." Two years earlier, I would have begged for this scenario now in front of me. I now had three great coaching choices available when only two years earlier I had walked on the beach with Pauline, disconsolate and homesick for England.

I had been preparing to include Colin in the coaching staff at the Hotspurs had I stayed there as Director. Now I was leaning toward moving to the Nomads. After many hours of deliberation and debriefing Joe on the situation at MBSC, I made what was for me a surprising choice.

I learned that the German coach had been a disaster. If some of the mothers at MBSC didn't like me, they were appalled by the German coach's arrogant, male chauvinistic approach to these "soccer ignoramus women" – his words, not mine! It was also reported that he was overheard saying, "They should be at home in the kitchen cooking their husband's meals." Nobody can survive in California in any walk of life with those prejudiced views – especially in youth soccer. His infamous joke – "How many men does it take to pop off the top of a bottle of their beer? None. The women should have already done this for him bringing it to him from the refrigerator." In addition to his arrogance toward the mothers, he made no attempt to hide his contempt for Joe's English heritage and

Hank's "American ignorance." He was also disliked at the San Diego Sockers for his condescending attitude to his teammates.

In two years, with the cumulative effort of losing a group of star players who followed me to the Hotspurs and destructive coaching leadership, Mission Bay Soccer Club was on the brink of collapse. I still felt antipathy toward Joe and my mistrust of Hank was deeply ingrained.

I chose the Nomads!

However, I encouraged Hank to consider giving Colin the job as replacement for the now departed German coach. In fact, I drove Colin to the interview at the home of one of the mothers who had voted to fire me!

I said my sad farewells to the Hotspurs, especially Rex and his wife, Vickie, and readied myself for my new coaching job with the famous Nomads Club. Colin was hired by Hank at MBSC, and the pieces of the puzzle seemingly began to fit into place smoothly.

Colin joined Hank and John and he also took over my teaching job at Sacred Heart as I began to develop my real estate career. Joe had done a first class job of developing the Girls Soccer program at the University, and in truth, was happier and more committed to that than his job at Mission Bay. Despite Colin's great playing ability and experience, his teaching and coaching ability was very weak. He lacked drills and teaching technique, often showing lack of adult leadership skills and role model qualities to his students.

Joe could have nurtured Colin, using his Head of Department experience from his teaching days in England. However, disaster struck for Joe when he was falsely accused of inappropriate behavior with one of his female university soccer team. Like all scandals, rumors abounded, and it was difficult to glean what was supposed to have occurred. Knowing Joe for twenty years, I found it hard to believe, and still do to this day, that he would be capable of unacceptable behavior toward any student. Amidst swirling controversy, it seems a deal was struck and he left San Diego and California for a youth soccer coaching job in the Midwest. Despite our difficulty, during my departure from Mission Bay, I was sickened to see the "rush to judgment." Several mothers in MBSC immediately turned nasty and accusatory without even knowing the facts. From being the original "nice guy," Joe left California under a cloud; an ignominious ending to a great new life in California for a genuinely nice guy.

All of Joe's friends and I had loved to make fun of him in a friendly way. He was good at being the butt of jokes and had a rapier like wit to respond. "Poor Joe. He has no luck. If he bought a toy dog, it would die." "If he fell in a barrel of tits, he would come up sucking his thumb." "Poor Joe. His mother wanted a boy!" The Joe who left California was not the livewire, carefree young man who had arrived only a few years earlier. He settled into his new coaching career and then was hired as the college coach of a prestigious small private college. Over the many years, he has done another first class job of developing both the boys and girls program at the college. I see him occasionally when he is in San Diego recruiting at the Surf Cup.

A few years ago, I heard that he had married a wonderful young lady, and even better news followed when they had a beautiful baby. The three of them visited my best mate, Tony, in Manchester, who had been a long time friend of Joe's from our teaching days in Salford, England. Tony told me how attractive Joe's wife was, the stunning beauty of the baby, and the joy and love between Joe and his wife. In his fifties, he had found happiness, content-ment, and peace within a family of his own. It seemed that some sad stories can have a happy ending, even for him. Unfortunately a couple of years ago, Tony gave me the tragic news that Joe's wife had fallen ill with some form of cancer. Joe's bad luck returned, and his wife died, leaving him, at nearly sixty years of age a widower and father of an adorable infant

The Nomads 1987 – 1990 – Two Stubborn Englishmen

I threw myself into my new job, anxious to impress my new boss, Derek, who was now a nationally recognized and respected coaching figure. Ironically, his friend and assistant, Brian, had taken over the college job left vacant by Joe's hasty departure. Derek was the head coach of the men's program at the same college. This was my first coaching job in the United States where I was not the man in charge. In hindsight, it was obvious that with two obstinate, working class Englishmen working together; it would not be smooth sailing.

Derek was, and still is, a dour, determined little man who has achieved great success at the highest level of American Youth Soccer. Fortunately for him, he had two superb partners who have helped greatly to smooth over his rough edges. His wife, Mary, is a "saint," fantastic mother, grandmother, and supportive wife whatever the circumstance. Derek's assistant, Brian, a superb coach, totally loyal partner, and protector of "Derek's back." Allen Field in La Jolla is an "ideal soccer facility" with a nice, comfortable clubhouse, excellent fields, and stunning views across the canyon to the crystal blue Pacific Ocean. Also noticeable to me was the number of elegant, attractive mothers dropping their boys off in the car park. On game day, every home sideline boasted stunning ladies in expensive casual attire with young, virile, athletic soccer coaches teaching soccer to the sons of these ladies. The ingredients for scandal were already in place.

Using the same field on different days was a semi-competitive local club, The La Jolla Lazers. Not in any real sense competition for the Nomads, the Lazers' players were nearly all La Jolla residents, whereas many Nomads players were from all over San Diego County. Head Coach of the Lazers was a European gentleman with immaculate hair, perfect coaching attire, and a suave demeanor. I played some pick up soccer games with him and realized he was much show and little substance. I noticed his desire to impress his older girls teams, but as he was a single man, this vanity was understandable. The Lazers' program was really a dormant giant waiting for a real shot of energy.

The shot, when it came for the Lazers, came suddenly and without warning when their head coach was arrested for having sex with one of his underage female soccer players. He was gone and his pleasant life in and around the upscale La Jolla community was over. I was told that his hair turned white over the following tumultuous months as he faced huge attorney fees for himself and the parents of the young lady, as well as psychiatric counseling for them all. He received prison time, and I believe he was deported back to his own country.

I was busy at the Nomads trying to strengthen a very average Under 12 boy's team and attempted to recruit TK. When I left the Hotspurs, Bob, TK's dad, had moved him much nearer to their home in Del Mar to the San Diego Surf Club – the Nomad's biggest opponents! TK's Surf Team reached the State Cup Final, but Bob was unhappy with the level of coaching from the Surf's volunteer coach. They lost in the final, and I managed to recruit not only TK but several other good players from his Surf team, much to the disgust of the Surf Club and its Head Coach!

After six years of heavy involvement in the San Diego Youth Soccer scene, I was now well known and had a large number of contacts. Recruiting was beginning to take place on a more frequent basis, especially between Surf and the Nomads. Having added the Surf players, I also managed to go back to the Hotspurs team and recruit a super goalkeeper, Beau, and an exceptional attacker. From mediocre, I now had a squad of talented players. The final "jewel in the crown" appeared during my Soccer Camps in Bakersfield when I acquired an outstanding player, Charlie Lynch. He was a great player from a wonderful family. They came to San Diego to see my Nomads team and agreed to have him play EVERY WEEK on my team in San Diego. This would necessitate a weekly round trip of 470 miles. True commitment!

The season began, and my team played attacking soccer with style and finesse. We were small and lacked great speed, but we moved well as a unit, and had many smart players and a first class goalkeeper. As the season moved on, my older team was solid, and I enjoyed the lack of pressure from coaching a "B" team. My younger U/12 team was now being noticed around Southern California and we approached the State Cub with some optimism. One negative was the behavior of several of the fathers on the team. I was to learn from experience that much of the parental problems come from the wealthier, affluent part of any team. Used to saying what they want and getting what they want, a humble soccer coach was not going to get in their way. With two high-powered surgeons and an extremely successful financial expert standing next to me on the sideline, the battle for power and control was fierce. Fortunately, the Nomads Club was not intimidated by parents, nor could it be bought. I was young, confident, and I was on a crusade! Lucky for me, I had Bob once again at my side now as my team manager. The more I got to know Bob, the more I got to respect his intelligence and management skills. Together we were a dynamic force determined to move the team to National prominence.

When we began State Cup, there were several teams that had dominated the Tournament in past years, and on reaching the quarter finals, we faced one of them – the State Champions from the previous year. They had an Asian player who looked to be around 15 years of age instead of twelve! With huge legs, blazing speed, and total confidence in himself, he was a one-man threat throughout the game. With us pressing the ball around neatly and our opponents launching long balls to Rocket Man, the game was a fascinating clash of styles. With only a few minutes, we were tied 0-0, thanks in great part to Bakersfield Charlie Lynch's defending and our goalkeeper Beau. With only a few minutes to go, we scored a neatly executed goal and hung on to win.

The semi-final was a success when we won handily 3-1 and advanced to the State Cup Final.

Despite my many years of show business work in England, my nerves were frayed as I drove on my own to Los Angeles for the Final. I was singing along with Anne Murray's "Daydream Believer" when I had to pull the car over to the side of the road. I was feeling nauseous as I contemplated the upcoming game. I had watched our upcoming opponents in their semi-final and was positive that we were the better skilled team. However, they were big, physical and aggressive. My main concern during the season was our lack of height and power.

The game began and within minutes, the other team, as I expected, were throwing themselves into tackles, then launching long balls over our defense. We were nervous, and I was probably the cause. Usually I would be joking with my players before a game. This day, I turned up with my game face on as though I was playing myself in the game.

As a spectacle, the game was poor and dragged on without any goals. Late in the second half, they scored a scrappy goal and their sideline went crazy. Beating a

Nomads team was always a big deal. Beating a Nomads team in the State Cup Final was the ultimate. I never like to lose, but to lose to a team of thugs was driving me crazy.

Throughout the game, I had continually begged the referee to control and punish the other team for dirty play. As the minutes raced by, we continued to trail 1-0. Bob told me to relax and try to communicate calmly to our players so they could begin to get into our usual rhythm of a calm, controlled passing game. It worked! I shouted to my team to ignore the score and try to play quality soccer for the last few minutes of the game. Almost immediately, we began to stroke the ball around and with our opponents visibly tiring, we got the ball into their penalty box. Our forward was clearly tripped and I looked at the referee, screaming for a penalty. Throughout the game I felt he had been far too lenient. This time, thankfully, he blew his whistle and pointed to the penalty spot. TK placed the ball down and calmly stepped back and waited for the whistle. Honestly, I had accepted that it was not our day and fate favored the "Hackers." Should we miss this penalty, I knew it was over for us. TK ran to the ball and calmly punched the ball with the side of his foot into the corner of the net. Tied ball game!

There were only two minutes to go to the end of the game. The other team was devastated and seemed to visibly fade. We attacked again, and unbelievably one of their players lunged at our forward, missed the ball, and knocked him over. A blatant penalty! But would the referee have the courage to give a second penalty within two minutes? He seemed to hesitate, and in that second, my loudest parent, Jim, shouted out ferociously, "He better give that or else." Hardly poetry, but it seemed to galvanize the referee who slowly pointed again to the spot.

Now I had a dilemma. Should TK take another penalty so soon? He always placed the ball in the same corner so maybe the goalkeeper would guess ahead. My right forward, Seth, was a very calm, skilled player with a mature disposition. Calmly I asked him, "Seth, do you want to take it?" I saw the look of hope and relief on TK's face. Seth nodded and composed as ever, easily scored. As soon as they kicked off, the referee blew the whistle and it was over!

Pandemonium broke out as our parents rushed onto the field. Before I could move, a hand grabbed my arm firmly. I turned and looked into the angry face of one of my player's mother.

"I hope you are happy now!!" she hissed. Her son was one of my weaker players and had only played a couple of minutes in the game. Throughout the season, we had several meetings regarding her son's playing time, and I had offered to release him or move him into our B team. The boy was happy on our team and didn't want to move.

"I'm ecstatic for ALL my players and parents. If you care to look on the field, you will see your son out there celebrating with joy," I replied, pulling my arm away from her grasp. Bob, seeing what had happened, came over and hugged me. He was a great team manager, who had done me the honor of him and TK staying with me through Mission Bay, Hotspurs, and now Nomads.

As I write this book 20 years later, ironically I can look out my window in Del Mar and almost see Bob's beautiful home a few hundred yards away.

In one season, with heavy recruiting, I had taken an average Nomads team to a State Cup Championship.

When the tryouts rolled around, success begets success and 85 boys turned up at Allen Field to try out for the best team in California. As good as my team was, I had several weaker players and told Derek I intended cutting them from the squad. He was adamant that my weakest player could not be dropped from the team. His father was the Nomads' attorney and an influential member of the La Jolla Community. "With your team you will be winning most games easily anyway, so why can't you put Chris on anyway?" Derek asked. At the time I was furious.

"Because he's nowhere near good enough to hold his own in the team," I replied.

"He's staying!" Derek shouted and stormed out of the clubhouse. The boy stayed!

Many years later, having dealt with similar situations with me as Head Coach, I smile, knowing how right Derek was. Besides soccer talent, there are many other factors, some political, which come into placing a child on a team. I will deal with them in a later chapter in this book.

I met with the throng of parents, thanking them for bringing their sons to try out for our team. Out of fairness, I explained that I would not necessarily choose the best eight at the tryouts. First, I always like to leave one or two spots should a "super star" appear. A few months later, I was really happy that I had. Secondly, I explained, I was only looking for "impact players" who could improve the starting lineup.

Unknown to me at the time, one of the fathers at that meeting, a judge, was to preside over a settlement meeting I was involved in years later regarding a real estate commission. He must have liked the speech. He awarded me the settlement money.

At the end of the try out, I had added two great players, Damon from the Hotspurs and Bryan from another nearby Club. We were ready for the next season knowing we would be the target for everybody to aim at. "Heavy lies the crown."

A stunning phone call started my day when I received

a message from Colin saying that Mission Bay Soccer Club had folded. I had incredibly mixed feelings with anger toward Hank still hanging with me. Yet, the thought of that Club disappearing with all my great memories left me somewhat depressed. The temptation to gloat was strangely absent as I digested this bombshell. What would Hank do now? His "baby" was gone. His complete social life and many hours a week now unfulfilled. Little did I know that Hank and I would be inextricably linked for many years to come.

Colin was now out of a job and asked me if I could put in a good word for him at the Nomads. Fortunately, he was hired, with Derek, the Head Coach, little realizing how much "double trouble" he now had on his coaching staff. I was happy to have Colin working beside me on the same field and around to mentor him - to smooth his rough edges. He continued to work for me at my summer camps, and we still spent many hours socializing.

After only eight years living in America and experiencing first-hand the early birth of competitive youth soccer, I now felt that I was a much better soccer coach. I had earned a decent reputation in both the San Diego Soccer community and hopefully Southern California as well.

In truth, I was blind to the number of parents along the way who I had upset and who were now consequently "enemies in waiting."

During one game in La Jolla, a mother from the other team, stormed over to me after a game, where we had beaten her son's team 6-0.

"You and your team are a disgrace! You embarrassed our team, by running up the score, and your team are MEAN and NASTY!" she fumed. Then she flounced away.

I discovered later that night that she and her husband

were close friends of my good mate, Bob. She had phoned him that afternoon, knowing Bob's son was a Nomad player. Bob was laughing out loud, when he called to inform me of his conversation with my recent "enemy." She had called him to ask if he knew the "Obnoxious English Pig who coached at the Nomads." True to form, Bob told her he did and I was "Even worse than she described!!!"

Over the following years, unbeknownst to her, I became good friends with her husband who swam at the same health-club as me – small world!

The Nomads 1989 – 1990; Success, Failure, Controversy

I felt that my early success at the Nomads was not greeted with the amount of thanks and gratitude I deserved. However, I was already realizing Derek was not the world's jolliest man. My sardonic comment was that "Derek had been banned from funerals because of depressing other people." Nevertheless, he was inarguably the boss of one of America's top competitive youth soccer clubs. The older Nomads teams especially were of the very highest quality, with many of San Diego's finest players inexorably drafting into the Nomads Club.

One of the Nomads finest players was a young man, J.J. Kinsell, who was a striker with incredible speed. He was a great character who was loved by all and made friends easily. It was with extreme sadness when the news traveled through the Nomads team that he had been killed in a motorcycle accident. I was in a state of disbelief. Two great young men killed from the same soccer club within a few years of each other. Again, I reflected how much more was my involvement as a professional youth soccer coach than just a teacher of the sport.

The funeral was incredibly sad with many of JJ's friends and teammates openly crying and unable to deal with their grief. Derek was heartbroken as if he had lost a member of his own family – in some ways, maybe he had.

A quarter of a century later, JJ's memory lives on thanks to a donation of land from his family to the Nomads Club. "Kinsell" Soccer Facility is a superb soccer field, ten minutes away from the Nomad's home facility in La Jolla. Just recently, the Argentinean National Team, including Leonel Messi, used Kinsell Field to train before their international game against the USA.

Colin's arrival at the Nomads had not gone unnoticed by the mothers within the club, and Colin did not go around with his eyes closed either. He was now divorced from his wife, single, and fancy free. We together were "free spirits" within a Nomads organization that reflected Derek's stodgy, dictatorial style. Brian, his partner, brought style and substance to the leadership of the club. In the early 1980's when the Club benefactor, Joe Hollow, stopped financing the club with his own money, Derek had been forced to reinvent the financial side of the club. He had survived and deserved credit for keeping the Nomads moving forward at the highest level.

With my "Championship" team now strengthened, we approached our first games in great spirits with team morale high.

I still had to deal with loud, outspoken dads who couldn't keep their mouths shut or their opinions to themselves. The loudest of them all was Jim, a surgeon, who had the loudest voice I have ever heard and the least soccer knowledge I have ever seen. If ignorance is bliss, Jim was blissfully happy. On the field he was truly a buffoon – a likable one. All these dads believed they knew the secret to successful soccer, despite the fact they had never played and were not great athletes themselves. They were all successful businessmen who lived in beautiful homes. Fortunately for me, all their sons were great soccer players and wonderful boys.

Part way through the season, I was hearing great things about a boy named Jovan Kirovski who was playing for an older team in Escondido, 20 miles away from La Jolla. He was actually the correct age for my team but was playing in his own neighborhood, one year up. In November, his team's season ended and many of them went off to tryouts for high school teams. I had one roster spot open on my team, and I had been trying to recruit a great player from our arch-enemy, the Bonita Rebels. Scot Shields, Jr. was a tall, tough player who had always impressed me during our many battles against the Rebels. His father, Scott Sr., was the team coach and had given me a few little encouraging signs that his son MAY be available to join us.

One dark November night, a short, powerful gentleman walked up to me and introduced himself politely at the Nomads field.

"My name is Zivko Kirovski. I was hoping you would be willing to give my son a tryout for your team. His name is Jovan, and he has been playing for an older team where we live in Escondido." I looked at his son who was standing a few yards away, quietly and politely looking at me and his father.

"Yes, I would be delighted to see him play. I have heard great reports about him from many sources," I said. I held out my hand and shook both father's and son's hands, feeling something special was about to happen – a sense of anticipation.

I introduced Jovan to the team and we started practice. After half an hour, I could see that he was a very good player, but he seemed to be holding back.

"Is there a problem, Jovan? You seem to be unwilling to play physically or with much aggression?" I asked gently.

"No coach. I just don't want to cause any problems or upset any of your players by tackling too hard in training."

My impression was he was a truly nice, young man, which still remains true to this day despite the great success that has come his way since that first night. I encouraged Jovan to play as if it were a Cup Final and not worry about the other players' views. He was stunning! For the next hour, his balance, skill, vision, and strength were breathtaking. Surrounded by one of the best group of players in the USA, he stood out like a crown jewel. Here, surely was my final piece of the puzzle. Ironically, Scott Shields Jr. was to go on to have a successful career in the NFL and Jovan would go on to play for Manchester United and the USA National team and is still playing now in the Major League Soccer.

With Jovan signed for our team, we approached our Nomads Thanksgiving Tournament in a confident mood. I had encouraged Derek in my early days at the Nomads to offer a Tournament using our National reputation as a springboard. Ironically, I was at his house one day when he introduced me to a gentleman he had brought in from Dallas to advise him on setting up a Tournament. The English gentleman had enormous experience, running the top Tournament in the United States. Unfortunately, we both knew each other and were mortal enemies!

In 1980, while still living in England, I had brought my All-Star City Team from Salford to compete in the prestigious Dallas Cup. After a year of intense fundraising, I had managed to bring my group of talented soccer players to the USA to compete. A group of inner-city boys, many from socially deprived homes, this Tour to Dallas USA was a trip of a lifetime. This Englishman in front of me at Derek's house had done as much as he could to ruin that trip ten years earlier! It's a small world. It certainly is! As we faced each other, Jon Preston was dumbstruck to be facing somebody he never thought he would encounter again in his life.

When my best mate and coaching partner, Tony Moore, and I arrived with our team in Dallas in 1980, we met the Tournament Director, Jon Preston, who was an Englishman, originally from Blackpool, a nearby neighborhood city 50 miles from Salford. Happy to meet a fellow

Englishman, Tony and I shook Jon's hand with enthusiasm. His lack of warmth and dour personality was a severe disappointment to both of us. Up to the start of the Dallas Cup, both Tony and I found him to be extremely cold and unwelcoming.

Real trouble blew up when we moved on from our group play, advancing to the quarter finals. We had lost one game 4-1 in our group play to a very strong, physical Dallas team. In the quarter final, we were to play the same team. This alone did not please Tony or me as we had already played them in group play.

When we arrived for our quarter final game, I noticed that one of their players was wearing a full arm cast. In fact, it was the player who had destroyed us in the previous game. I casually mentioned to my partner, Tony, about the opponent's cast. Tony, never a "shrinking violet," strode across the field to examine the opponent's cast. I could tell by his body language and the commotion surrounding the player that a serious problem was beginning to escalate. When he returned to our side of the field, Tony was fuming. "There is no fu..ing way we are going to play the game with that boy's arm wrapped in a lethal weapon," Tony insisted. I jogged over to take a look for myself. It was a full arm, solid plaster cast – hard as a rock – an accident waiting to happen.

The mood of the other coaches and their players was extremely antagonistic. I heard one cynical comment, "They're scared to let him play because he "toasted" them in the first game!" I had been fairly calm up to this point, but the comment rubbed me the wrong way.

"We welcome the chance to play you again. You beat us last game, deservedly. However, I am in charge of 18 boys who are 5,000 miles from their homes. If any of them got hit in the face and badly injured, I would be 'toast' for allowing the game to take place."

We obviously needed an impartial person to mediate and make a decision. "Cometh the hour, cometh the man." Jon Preston, Tournament Director Extraordinaire, was summoned to arbitrate. True to his track record with us so far, he showed little sympathy or warmth for our argument. "The Referee's decision will be final," he declared pompously and strode away. I had to restrain Tony from following him and administering the "Salford Kiss" (a head butt to the nose).

By now, the atmosphere was electric with barbed comments flying across the field. Our boys were totally pumped up to avenge our earlier defeat. That game had been played at 8:00 AM, an ungodly hour for English soccer players who never kick off before 10 AM. No excuses. Jet lag, early kick off, the other team were a year older - we lost fair and square!

Now we waited anxiously for the referee and linesmen to arrive to give a decision on the player with the cast. "What do we do if he says their guy can play?" I asked Tony. "There's no way he will support a player playing with such danger and liability at stake," Tony replied confidently. He was wrong!

The referee agreed to allow the opponent to play, cast and all. We were cornered. Our boys were now confused and we were in a situation neither of us had ever encountered. All our hard work, fundraising, travel, and practice were at stake. The other team was openly gloating, which did nothing to lighten my mood or Tony's. Finally, reluctantly, we decided on safety grounds, and truthfully, in hindsight, in an anti-Jon Preston gesture, to forfeit the game. Again, Tony was looking for Preston's head. To avoid possible future incidents, we gathered our players and drove away from the field, all with a huge sense of anti-climax.

Almost ten years later, I was surprised to find that my feelings toward Jon Preston were still as bitter as ever. I looked at him and said, to Derek, "Sorry, I didn't realize you were busy. I'll call you later," and walked out. Later that day, I saw Derek at the Nomads Field. "My God. I wondered what the hell was going on. That was the most embarrassing moment I have ever experienced," Derek whined. Knowing Derek's penchant for bluntness, I found his statement somewhat hard to believe.

"Sorry Derek. There are few people in the world that I despise. Jon Preston is one of them," I replied. I then put two and two together. Both Derek and Preston were from the same city in England. Both had grumpy personalities, and both were small men in stature. A match made in heaven. (I do truly like Derek – for all his foibles.)

Nomads Thanksgiving Tournament – Trouble!!!

On the Friday after Thanksgiving, I arrived at Allen Field, ready for our first game against a bitter rival from Irvine. The bitterness was on their side, not ours. We had beaten them on several occasions and had never lost to them. My mate, Colin, was coaching five minutes away at Cliffridge Field, and I had dropped him off earlier.

As game time approached, the warm up was coming to an end, and the referees started the pre-match check in for both teams. Suddenly our team manager was unable to find our players' game ID cards. Somebody mentioned that they saw Pete, one of the other team managers, pick up the team manager's bag and head off to Cliffridge Field. In hope and desperation, one of my parents ran off to try and retrieve our cards. Game time was closing in and their coach suddenly declared that they would be enforcing the check in rules to the second. In eight minutes they would take the game as forfeit. I was furious! "You are kidding me!!" You travel 100 miles each way, and now you would prefer to steal the points rather than wait a few minutes and play the game," I exploded. With a sneer on his fat, ugly face, he responded, "Correct."

Derek appeared when he got word that trouble was brewing. Trying to defuse the situation, he tried to reason with the Irvine coach. That was a waste of time. As the seconds ticked by, the mood grew more and more volatile. With literally seconds to go and the Irvine coach looking at his watch continually to annoy me I'm sure, the parent came running through the gate with the cards!!! Game on!!

Realizing my mood and severe antipathy toward the opposing coach, Derek suggested that he coach my team for that one game. In all the 28 years I have known Derek, that was probably the smartest, most insightful thing he has ever come up with. Unfortunately, I was having none of it. I wanted to beat this coach and his team 10-0 and relish every second if it! Reluctantly, Derek agreed that I could coach the "needle" game.

After only a few minutes against the run of play, the other team scored. Their coach's scream of joy could be heard all over the Field. It was a dagger in my heart. I would willingly lose the League or a Cup Final rather than lose to this "tosser."

As the game wore on, we were in complete control but they fought hard to keep their lead. Then Jovan scored. I have never jumped so high. "Not before time!!! We deserve it!!!" I taunted looking across at the burly figure of the Irvine coach. A few minutes later, we scored again. VICTORY! Vindication! I wished it had been more decisive, but we had won.

Then came an incident which convinced me that the lining up of players and coaches at the end of the game to "high five" each other is often ill advised, especially after a tense game. Was this an accident waiting to happen? As both teams crossed each other giving "high fives," I was at the back, in the customary place for a coach.

When all the players had finished the final handshake, the other coach and I faced each other. "Thanks for the game," I said coldly, holding out a floppy hand. "Go f.ck yourself, you limey bastard," was the inflammatory response. I turned, and as I walked away, came back with an adlib from my old days in show business:

"Fat, ugly, foul-mouthed, and a bad loser – what a great combination!"

Next I heard him bellow, and I heard footsteps racing toward me. Turning around I saw my nemesis now only a few yards away and closing fast. I stood there in a state of shock. Unsure what to do, I could not start running away.

Instinctively I stepped forward, grabbed his neck in a headlock, and tripped his legs to restrain him. As he fell, I fell on top on him. Still with his neck trapped in my right arm, looking up, I saw one of his parents, built like an NFL linebacker, racing toward us. Not a good way to spend Thanksgiving weekend! Their coach was a solid guy, but the parent racing toward us was huge. I hesitated whether to stay on the ground or jump up. I decided that jumping up may make the parent feel like I was going to fight him. Also, I doubted that the parent would jump on top of me or try to kick me. "Let him go right now," implored the huge parent in a surprisingly gentle voice. By now, my head was clearing and I was wondering what I was doing on the ground with a man's head locked in my arm.

The players must have been terrified and both sets of parents mortified. I got up and released my opponent, and strangely, without words, we walked away from each other. Embarrassed, I stuttered out an explanation of sorts and an apology for what had transpired.

Making a hasty retreat, I jumped in my car and headed to pick Colin up. After a short ride, I arrived at Cliffridge Field and found Colin seemingly hiding behind a wall. He dashed out to the car and jumped in telling me to drive off immediately. "What's going on?" I asked.

"A nightmare!" Colin replied nervously. I wondered if he had heard about my debacle and was referring to me. "I've just had a nasty incident during the last game. One of their players injured one of mine with a filthy tackle. I ran on to the field to attend to my player and ran past the dirty bastard who was himself still on the ground. Their players were at me and tried to trip me as I ran past him. As I took evasive action, I tripped and accidentally stepped on him. All hell broke loose. The Cerritos team was all Hispanic and it felt like a racist war about to explode. Let's go!"

I suddenly realized I had left my bag of soccer balls and cones back at Allen Field, so I returned to pick them up. As I entered the car park, I saw two police cars, and then I heard, "There he is!" I looked toward the Clubhouse and saw a crowd of parents, three policemen, and my "sparring partner" all looking in my direction.

"What the hell is going on?" Colin asked.

"More of the same as you," I replied.

As I approached the group, my adversary pointed to me and shouted, "Arrest him!" I thought that maybe I was on Candid Camera. One of the policemen told me that I was under arrest. Colin was relieved that he was no longer the center of attention and looked on in dismay.

"Under arrest for what?" I asked incredulously.

"For assaulting me," chimed in big mouth.

"You were the one who rushed at me after using foul and obscene language. What did you expect me to do? Run away?"

At this point, one of my player's parent stepped forward – one of many attorneys in the Nomads Club. "I saw the whole incident. The Irvine coach ran at our coach in a threatening manner. Jeff did no more than protect himself. If Jeff is to be arrested, then he can make a citizen's arrest on his accuser." It sounded professional and authoritative. My opponent lost his composure at the thought of being arrested. The police were obviously frustrated by this petty bickering between two grown men. "Alright both of you are arrested, unless you both agree to drop the charges against each other," threatened the police sergeant. Finally common sense prevailed and everybody dispersed. Colin and I went for a meal, and we exchanged our war stories for an hour or so.

The next morning I arrived at the field for a game and

was delighted to see my favorite coach from Irvine sporting a beautiful black eye! I discovered later that he had upset a man at the San Diego Sockers Indoor game the previous evening. Obviously, he had upset the wrong man! The sad part for me was the fact that he had his own son on the team and was a volunteer coach. For the son to experience all this on a regular basis must have been very traumatic for the youngster.

England, soccer are in his blood

By JOSIE KARP, Staff Writer

T.K. Inbody was not sure where his last name came from. It turns out, the surname has English derivations. It makes sense.

When he was 14, Inbody packed up and moved to Prestwich, England, just outside Manchester, to live five months with a family he had met on a previous trip to England. He hung out with new friends and went to pubs.

He also played soccer.

Inbody

Inbody, 18, is the center midfielder on the Torrey Pines soccer team, last year's CIF-San Diego Section Division II champions. He did not arrive in the middle of the field on one of the best teams in the county by mistake.

When Inbody decided after the eighth grade that he would spend part of the next year in England, even if that meant repeating the school year, the trip was about more than taking on new challenges, overcoming obstacles, and having fun. It was about becoming a better soccer player.

Inbody went back to Prestwich again last summer. This time, he played on a semipro team, with local players who ranged in age from 18-30.

The work appears to be paying off. Torrey Pines, ranked fifth in the county in the coaches' poll, is in good shape to defend its title — the Falcons own an Avocado League best 7-0-2 record.

The Falcons' two ties, their only blemishes in league play so far, both came on the road.

"The biggest problem we have in away games is that we have a field where you can knock the ball around and use your skills," said Torrey Pines coach Brian McManus. "Sometimes you have to go to certain fields and just play ugly soccer."

Fields that have been beaten up by rain or with ditches at midfield and dirt around the goal. Inbody endured conditions like that in England. The trip to Ramona, he can handle. And if you want to play physical, Inbody can do that, too.

"The style of play (in England) is a little different," said Inbody. "They have good skills but I think it's more athletic oriented. It's more running, and more strength."

What Inbody does best, though, is handle the ball. "He does things with the ball at times that you can't explain," said McManus. "There are times when it looks like the ball is attached to T.K.'s feet."

At other times, says McManus, it also looks like he might be losing his head.

"He's really a highly emotional kid," said McManus. "He plays very emotionally. He hates to get beat. He always thinks he can do better. Without that emotion, without that drive, he'd just be another ordinary player."

Inbody has not fallen into that category yet. With a scholarship offer from Stanford and Yale still courting him, Inbody probably won't be called ordinary any time soon.

Darren Fanelli
Franchise player #1

TK Inbody
Franchise player #3

These Nomads Made Their Point

■ Soccer: The coach is boasting about the program, but after the way the under-14 team played in the Dallas Cup, he has good reason.

By JOHN GEIS
TIMES STAFF WRITER

SAN DIEGO—Boy, Jeff Illingworth has some nerve.

He has only been coach of the La Jolla Nomads' under-14 team for two years, and already he is touting the soccer program as "without a doubt, the most highly successful in America."

Well, maybe it is. One would certainly be hard pressed to find anyone with whom to argue the point.

If the Nomads didn't already have a pretty good idea about their standing among American soccer clubs, their egos certainly were not diminished by the fact that foreign competitors at last month's Dallas Cup were offering as much as $18 for "Nomads" pins.

Yup, thanks to the Nomads, U.S. youth soccer has gone from doormat status to status symbol.

While at Dallas Cup XI, however, the Nomads weren't just playing the part of young entrepreneurs. The under-14 club busied itself with winning the championship.

So maybe Illingworth isn't so full of gall after all.

The Nomads beat up a team from Sweden, 9-0, skimmed by a team from Peru, 1-0, and went up against Club America, a Mexican squad considered one of the top youth programs in the world.

Nomad players will tell you they were outplayed in that one, but they will also mention that they managed to outscore Club America, 1-0.

"No, we didn't outplay them," admitted T.K. Inbody, one of the team captains.

"But it was a tight game," said Bryan Sproviero, one of the team's top two goal scorers.

It was not so tight in the final, where the Nomads made the Detroit Wolves, an Olympic development squad, look like just another U.S. soccer team, 5-1.

With that victory, the under-14 Nomads became the only U.S. side to win a championship in Dallas. There were three other age divisions, and Nomad teams advanced to at least the quarter-finals in each.

But it wasn't *that* the under-14 team won that impressed onlookers as much as *how* they won it.

Paul Gardner, a columnist for Soccer America, wrote this in his weekly column:

"I have watched a good many Nomads teams over the past few years, and have always found them . . . lacking in sophistication. But the U-14 Nomad boys were a delight to behold, with the courage and the confidence to repeatedly *play* the ball out of defense on the ground."

Thank you very much for

noticing, says Illingworth, who despises the conventional U.S. coaching wisdom of molding a team around the athletic attributes of a few stars.

Illingworth would rather mold players into a team.

"It's not a question of consciously teaching a strategy," he said, "but we do tend to play more of a South American style. We play as a team, but with a lot of individual skill."

The Nomads play so much of a South American style that Gardner attributed their success to the fact that "they had Hispanic players in key positions." But the Nomads' midfield—shouldered with the responsibility of engineering the attack—consists of Inbody, Seth Doros, Craig Markley and Jovan Kirovski. None are Hispanic.

Instead, the tactical game is attributable to Illingworth, the coach himself said.

"Because that's how I played," he explained. "I stress sound, one-touch passing."

Said Gardner: "They were much more thoughtful in their attack. A lot of American teams just hit the ball up the field. The Nomads were playing it up. I didn't see any evidence on this team of the ball being whacked upfield and the players scurrying about to catch up with it."

The Nomads' attack—often finished by Sproviero and Ivan Aguilar, each of whom scored five goals in the six games at Dallas—deserves second billing in Illingworth's mind. It was the defense, mainly goalie Beau Sager, that allowed the team to advance to the championship. Sager allowed just three goals in the six games.

"He may be the best goalie in California," Illingworth said. "He had a major impact."

The defenders in front of Sager included three state Olympic development team members: Damon Bradshaw, Robert Crawford and Charlie Lynch.

With that many players on the Olympic development squad, it would appear the Nomads are doing a fine job developing future players for the U.S. national team. But Illingworth doubts many Nomads will play at that level . . . or professionally.

It's a matter of economics. While one trend in soccer here is the continual upgrading of young players' skills, another is that the players themselves come from wealthy backgrounds.

Illingworth estimates the average family income of his 19 players approaches $250,000.

U.S. national team members make $28,000. Average players in England pull down $30,000. Average indoor players earn around $40,000.

"But these players [the Nomads] have other things to look forward to," Illingworth said.

Photos by SEAN M. HAFFEY / For The Times
Bryan Sproviero (left) is one of the Nomads' top two goal scorers.

Defender Robert Crawford dribbles upfield at a Nomad practice.

Jeff Illingworth
(author)

New to America
Just arrived in 1981

1960 - Manchester, England
Alfred Street, Elementary School

1979 - Manchester, England
Like father, like son

Jeff Illingworth and older son:
Danny

younger son:
Ben

Jeff and family during happy times

honestly, they are happy...

Soccer's age of innocence

The kids having fun and the parents relaxed
(pre-desperation)

Jeff and his players visiting
Manchester United's stadium - The Theater of Dreams

Truly a "Happy Jack"
Jack Dempsey & Manchester United Superstar, Wayne Rooney

Fantastic aerial view of the prestigious Surf Cup

Dynamic action at the surf cup

A difficult prize to attain... only the "best of the best"

Chugger scoring with his head

Chugger the goal machine!

...p would bring the season
...nting one. However, the
...ral teams to the Dallas Cup,
...ks after State Cup ends. My team
...entered, and I heard Manhattan
...competing. Lifting ourselves back up
...challenge, and I tried to make practice
...ting:

...been told he would be going to Dallas with
...nt. He had started to talk about a career as
...interesting because he had no advanced
...left school at 16 years of age to play pro-
...also had no flying experience whatso-
...math and science. I pointed out to
...st 25 years of study to qualify as a
...he liked the pilot uniform, and as
...crew were gay, he would have
...line stewardesses. His lack of
...on become crystal clear.
...'s players and parents were
...rth Airport four hours after
...oaches had flown in. We
...uses and Derek instruct-
...players and parents a
...the mini-bus and
...irport. I sa
...t to Co...

...e easy,
...sion of
...g game
...inst an
...st a team
...e against
...match that
...team was
...to play for
...ncing to the
...d noted that

...coaching col-
...at Dallas night
...ment seemed to
...rs seemed to be
...with their sons.
...ittle heed to their
...e soccer coaches.
...ntense soccer, fol-

Defending the State Cup Title – No Easy Task

With Jovan, Bryan Sproveiro and Damon Bradshaw added to our previous State Cup Championship Team, we had a Dream Team! Going through the season, we were rarely tested and the team continued to grow in confidence. As the State Cup approached, expectations were high and I was proud to be the coach of such a talented group of young soccer players.

We cruised through the group games scoring freely, and I was able to play all the players in every qualifying game. The semi-final and final games were to be played in Bakersfield, necessitating a four hour drive each way. I hitched a ride with Bob and TK and we drove north through Los Angeles over the Grapevine mountain to Bakersfield.

On that Saturday, our semi-final was to be played first so we would have the advantage of watching the other semi-finals. As a coach, there is no better feeling than looking at your starting 11 seeing no weakness and huge talent. For our sweeper, Charlie Lynch, it was a home game – he lived in Bakersfield! The game itself was very competitive, but we always had an edge, and barring a freak goal, we always looked likely to win. At the final whistle, it was 2-1 for us and we were heading to our second consecutive State Cup Final!

I stayed to watch the other semi-finals and was not impressed or intimidated by what I saw. The winners were Manhattan Beach, and I felt confident that we were a much better side than them.

The next day I arrived at the field relaxed and very confident – very different from my mood at the Final the previous year. The players started to arrive in small groups and they seemed relaxed – maybe too relaxed! Several players actually arrived only 15 minutes before the game which did not please me too much. I started to have bad vibes about the game, and when we kicked off, I was unsettled and felt we were unprepared. How right I was.

We played really poorly and Sasha, the star player for the Manhattan Beach team, dominated the game. We deserved to lose, and we did 2-1. Everybody was stunned as we collected our losers' medals and began the long journey back to San Diego.

It was a miserable ride, but Bob, TK, and I finally came to the same conclusion. We had been too confident and were mentally unprepared to play the game. I was the coach and I had failed. It was a great lesson for me to take forward in my coaching career. There is a fine balance between nerves, adrenaline, and complacency in approaching big games. Too much of any of these emotions is counter-productive. Getting the right balance and communicating it to your team, is the ultimate challenge for the coach.

After the game I could sense and hear some of my moms and dads acutely surprised and disappointed by our surprise defeat. They were already desperately searching for excuses or somebody to blame! We had lost in the Final of America's toughest State Cup having won it the previous year. Surely, something to be proud of. The parents left the field, heads bowed, as though attending a funeral procession. We had lost a kid's soccer game!

knew we had missed
had not taken the DFW
reply was a classic.   "B
Terminal G, not DF or W!!"
taking the piss or what?" I aske
bemused face. "No. Why?" Col
stands for Dallas Forth Worth Airpor
you muppet!!!" When Colin realized h
we both started to howl with laughter.

The players and parents arrived and we
body from Terminal G in DFW Airport safely
Dallas Cup, and I was excited to be back, especially
great team.

It had been ten years since my first and last vi
Dallas Cup. In our group, we had an interesti
I was under no illusions that the games would b
and in fact, no Nomads team had ever won any div
The Dallas Cup. In our group, we had an interesti
to come against a team from India, one ag
American team, and a tough game for sure again
from a professional club in Mexico. The gam
India was a blowout win for us (11-0) in a mis
should never have taken place. The Americal
useful, but we won comfortably 3-1 and adva
the honor of winning our group and adva
quarter finals. I scouted the Mexican team an
we were going to have our hands full.

During the first couple of nights, my
leagues and I took full advantage of the gre
life. Parents of boys playing in the Tourna
be everywhere. A large number of mothe
the only parent to have made the trip
They were partying like crazy and paid
marital status, much to the delight of th
During the day it was high quality

lowed at night by late night drinking, dancing and singing.

The day of the game against our Mexican opposition, I sat the players down and seriously explained the task ahead of us. They were a professional team who trained full time, five days a week, and were very skilled. A weakness I had noted was their unwillingness to shoot from outside the penalty box. They liked to short pass, commit opponents, and then go around them. I asked my players not to over commit in the tackle or dive in. I asked them to follow the guy who passes the ball, and when we win possession, get the ball forward quickly to Damon and Bryan, our forwards.

The game was a battle with my players finding it difficult to get the ball from the Mexican players. When we had the ball, we lacked rhythm and cohesion, failing to create any real penetrating offence. Truthfully, we were second best, and I could not see us winning the game. Soccer is a fickle game and against the run of play, we were awarded a free kick just outside of their penalty area. To my intense relief, we scored and held on desperately until the final whistle.

The weather during the week had turned nasty and many games were postponed. We managed to find an available field for practice, and we drove out there on a large bus. Before leaving San Diego, Colin had jokingly chipped the ball at TK hitting him in the "nuts." TK had doubled up in pain and not found the joke that funny. As Colin walked down the steps of the bus, TK said, "Hey Colin!" As Colin turned, TK returned the favor, throwing a ball firmly and hitting Colin in his manhood. Colin almost fell down the stairs in pain as everybody laughed.

The weather caused a backlog of important games. The quarter-final was to be played at 7:00 PM the next evening, followed by the semi-final three hours later at

10:00 PM. Should we survive, the Final would be 14 hours later at noon the next day.

Our quarter-final game was played under lights against a street smart team from Peru, South America. They were clever, skillful, and cynical; committing several "professional" fouls I had rarely seen in my many years of coaching youth soccer. My parents were seething, and Jim, "the mouth," was screaming at every challenge delivered by the South American youngsters. Battered and bruised, we survived with a win.

With only two hours to the semi-final, rest and nourishment were the order of the day. Strangely, the other semi-final started at 8:000 PM, giving us one extra hour of rest and also a chance to scout our opponents. Both teams in the other semi-final were solid and capable, but not nearly as strong as the Mexican or Peruvian teams we had already played.

The winning team was from Northern California, and from my observation, they lacked speed in both full-back positions. I decided to change from our usual 4-4-2 formation to a more direct, attacking 4-3-3. Using two wide attacking players with great speed, we won the semi-final easily in what was something of an anti-climax after the "war" against Peru.

The Final was to be played against a well known team from Chicago who had won several tournaments around the nation during the past year. We were the underdogs, not even champions of our own State. The team that beat us in State Cup, Manhattan Beach, had not advanced out of their group.

As we warmed up before the Final, my thoughts traveled back ten years to the forfeit of my Salford boys team during their quarter final. Never in my wildest dreams did I believe I would be standing there, as coach of a

California team, warming up for this huge game. My old nemesis, Jon Preston, was no longer involved in The Dallas Cup, which was bittersweet for me. I was happy to hear he had left "under a cloud," but disappointed that he was not there to see my wonderful team in its finest hour.

The coach of the opposing team jogged over and held out his hand in a friendly manner, smiling pleasantly.

"What a great day. Congratulations on reaching the Final. You must be very pleased to have gotten this far," he said, in my mind, somewhat condescendingly. He continued in the same vein. "We just won the Florida National Tournament and are now unbeaten in any tournament in the past 18 months." I felt that he was trying to play mind games with me, and I was not too impressed with him physically or his approach.

"That's very impressive I must say. What's your own playing background in soccer?" I asked as I flicked the ball to him in the air. His response to the soccer ball arriving was to catch it. "Oh, you must have been a goalkeeper," I said dryly, noting that at 5'6" in height, it must have been a challenging task. As I walked away, I said in a humble voice, "I hope we can at least make this Final a challenging and worthwhile game for your team. We will try not to embarrass ourselves." My adrenaline was pumping and I gathered my players together for a spirited team talk.

"These guys are confident that they are going to whip our butts. They have little or no respect for us and think of us as a set of softies from the beaches of Southern California. Remember our over-confidence in the State Cup Final. Let's use this failing of theirs against them from the kick-off. In their faces, pressure them, and when we get the ball, quick one and two touch passing," I implored. Looking into the eyes of my players and watching their body language, I felt confident that we were ready and prepared.

I took my seat with my bench players at the side of the field. As luck would have it, my seat was about ten yards away from the Chicago coaches' bench. There was an atmosphere you could cut with a knife as the game kicked off.

From the first minute, it was clear to me that we were going to dominate the game as we passed the ball crisply with purpose. The goals game quickly with one of my two Hispanic players, Ivan (Hector) scoring two quick goals, followed by a third. I was buzzing and kept sneaking glances across at the opponent's bench. Instead of taking the high road, I loudly shouted to Colin at the other end of our bench,

"OK, let's get all the players off the bench and onto the field. This game is over!" This was childish and unprofessional, disrespectful to my own bench players I later realized and unnecessary. Within ten minutes of putting my five substitutes on the field, the score had narrowed to 3-2! Trying not to sound or look panicky or embarrass the subs, I quickly went back to the starting line-up. We rolled, unchallenged, through the remainder of the game, winning comfortably 6-3. When I shook the hand of the opposing coach, deadly silence reigned as we ignored each others' eyes. At least I didn't come out with some other inane, childish comments.

As with a previous final, as we celebrated, a mother and father came up to me to express their anger with me. "Why did you take our son off after only a few minutes? We have paid a fortune to come to this tournament and some players didn't pay a penny and played the whole game." They must have caught me at a bad moment because all I could answer was, "Get stuffed! I'm busy!" and ran away to celebrate with my team.

That night we all went to watch the Final of the U/19 Super Group, won again by a magnificent pro-Tahuichi team from South America. Unquestionably, the Super Group has no equivalent in any other Tournament. Over the years, many of the world's top pro clubs have invited U/19 teams in their elite Tournament.

My complaints with The Dallas Cup were the weather, fields spread everywhere, and a whole week stuck in a hotel room with those other coaches. Nevertheless, victory was sweet as all the coaches and parents went on a full-out celebration that lasted until the early hours of the morning.

Arriving back in San Diego late the next day, I proudly showed The Dallas Cup to my wife, Pauline, who had no interest in soccer and knew nothing about the significance of The Dallas Cup. This lack of involvement in my soccer coaching career, with its many days away at tournaments, was to eventually take a heavy toll.

A huge scandal erupted at a later Dallas Cup when a well known soccer coach was found guilty of altering the players cards to enable "ringers" to join the team during the tournament. The irony of the situation was that a "volunteer" parent was down on the roster as "Head Team Coach." In reality, this was a sham because the real team coach was ineligible to coach the team due to an NCAA College regulation. Consequently, the parent who was totally innocent was banned "sine die," and the coach who was the real culprit received a short ban and "flew under the radar."

Another coach was to also be involved in a problem with the U/20 National Team for naively encouraging a sick player to drink a "hot whisky with sugar" for medicinal purposes. As I mentioned at the beginning of this book, European coaches often ignore or don't comprehend the significant differences in U.S. laws about alcohol and under age sex. The net result was the coach lost the job working with the U.S. National Team - a shame because he was apparently doing a great job, and has contributed so much to U.S. Youth Soccer. In my years in youth soccer, it has been sad to see how many coaches and clubs have deliberately used overage players – sometimes for years! Where it is a player from another Country, that has difficulty producing birth certificates accurately, it sometimes produces situations where some players are obviously a year or more advanced physically. At times it is stunning to see the difference in the height, weight, and maturity of both boys and girls on the field in the top youth soccer tournaments. By the time college arrives, the later developer will often surprise many coaches, overtaking the early developers.

As with many youth soccer clubs, there was a huge amount of fraternizing between the male soccer coaches and the mothers of the players. This was especially true at the many tournaments where everybody stayed at the same hotel. The danger involved in these scenarios was to become very evident a few months after The Dallas Cup.

One of our coaches had become too close to the mother of one of our players and was flagrantly dating her. The husband was rarely, if ever, seen at the field or any games. He was apparently a quiet, retiring type of gentleman who worked as an engineer and kept himself to himself. I was intrigued by that since his wife was a dynamic lady who was extremely outgoing and opinionated. The coach and the mother made a dashing couple, and even the children seemed to accept it as normal that their mother and the coach were continually together. I often wondered what the father must be thinking with his wife rarely home and often away at summer soccer camps with their daughter.

Defending the State Cup Title – No Easy Task

With Jovan, Bryan Sproveiro and Damon Bradshaw added to our previous State Cup Championship Team, we had a Dream Team! Going through the season, we were rarely tested and the team continued to grow in confidence. As the State Cup approached, expectations were high and I was proud to be the coach of such a talented group of young soccer players.

We cruised through the group games scoring freely, and I was able to play all the players in every qualifying game. The semi-final and final games were to be played in Bakersfield, necessitating a four hour drive each way. I hitched a ride with Bob and TK and we drove north through Los Angeles over the Grapevine mountain to Bakersfield.

On that Saturday, our semi-final was to be played first so we would have the advantage of watching the other semi-finals. As a coach, there is no better feeling than looking at your starting 11 seeing no weakness and huge talent. For our sweeper, Charlie Lynch, it was a home game – he lived in Bakersfield! The game itself was very competitive, but we always had an edge, and barring a freak goal, we always looked likely to win. At the final whistle, it was 2-1 for us and we were heading to our second consecutive State Cup Final!

I stayed to watch the other semi-finals and was not impressed or intimidated by what I saw. The winners were Manhattan Beach, and I felt confident that we were a much better side than them.

The next day I arrived at the field relaxed and very confident – very different from my mood at the Final the previous year. The players started to arrive in small groups and they seemed relaxed – maybe too relaxed! Several players actually arrived only 15 minutes before the game which did not please me too much. I started to have bad vibes about the game, and when we kicked off, I was unsettled and felt we were unprepared. How right I was.

We played really poorly and Sasha, the star player for the Manhattan Beach team, dominated the game. We deserved to lose, and we did 2-1. Everybody was stunned as we collected our losers' medals and began the long journey back to San Diego.

It was a miserable ride, but Bob, TK, and I finally came to the same conclusion. We had been too confident and were mentally unprepared to play the game. I was the coach and I had failed. It was a great lesson for me to take forward in my coaching career. There is a fine balance between nerves, adrenaline, and complacency in approaching big games. Too much of any of these emotions is counter-productive. Getting the right balance and communicating it to your team, is the ultimate challenge for the coach.

After the game I could sense and hear some of my moms and dads acutely surprised and disappointed by our surprise defeat. They were already desperately searching for excuses or somebody to blame! We had lost in the Final of America's toughest State Cup having won it the previous year. Surely, something to be proud of. The parents left the field, heads bowed, as though attending a funeral procession. We had lost a kid's soccer game!

The Dallas Cup – A Mountain to Climb

Usually the Final of State Cup would bring the season to an end, albeit a disappointing one. However, the Nomads always send several teams to the Dallas Cup, which occurs several weeks after State Cup ends. My team was one of the teams entered, and I heard Manhattan Beach would also be competing. Lifting ourselves back up was an important challenge, and I tried to make practice intense but exciting.

Colin had been told he would be going to Dallas with us as our assistant. He had started to talk about a career as a pilot. This was interesting because he had no advanced education, having left school at 16 years of age to play professional soccer. He also had no flying experience whatsoever and very limited math and science. I pointed out to him that he had at least 25 years of study to qualify as a pilot. I secretly believed he liked the pilot uniform, and as most of the male cabin crew were gay, he would have unlimited access to the airline stewardesses. His lack of airline knowledge would soon become crystal clear.

A large group of Nomads players and parents were due to arrive at Dallas Fort Worth Airport four hours after Derek and I and all the other coaches had flown in. We went off site to pick up the mini-buses and Derek instructed us to go back to pick up the players and parents at Terminal G. "Captain" Colin drove the mini-bus and we headed back on the freeway to the airport. I saw a sign that said DFW Airport and indicated it to Colin. He told me to relax because we were not there yet. At the next DFW Airport sign, the same thing happened and we continued to speed along the freeway. The journey to the airport had now taken nearly 30 minutes, and we were leaving Dallas behind and heading out into the vast plains. I knew we had missed the airport and asked Colin why he had not taken the DFW exits. From an aspiring pilot, his reply was a classic. "Because Derek told us to go to Terminal G, not DF or W!!" I was incredulous. "Are you taking the piss or what?" I asked while looking at Colin's bemused face. "No. Why?" Colin asked. "Because DFW stands for Dallas Forth Worth Airport, Not Terminals DFW you muppet!!!" When Colin realized his massive blunder, we both started to howl with laughter.

The players and parents arrived and we ferried everybody from Terminal G in DFW Airport safely to our hotel. It had been ten years since my first and last visit to The Dallas Cup, and I was excited to be back, especially with a great team.

I was under no illusions that the games would be easy, and in fact, no Nomads team had ever won any division of The Dallas Cup. In our group, we had an interesting game to come against a team from India, one against an American team, and a tough game for sure against a team from a professional club in Mexico. The game against India was a blowout win for us (11-0) in a mismatch that should never have taken place. The American team was useful, but we won comfortably 3-1 and waited to play for the honor of winning our group and advancing to the quarter finals. I scouted the Mexican team and noted that we were going to have our hands full.

During the first couple of nights, my coaching colleagues and I took full advantage of the great Dallas night life. Parents of boys playing in the Tournament seemed to be everywhere. A large number of mothers seemed to be the only parent to have made the trip with their sons. They were partying like crazy and paid little heed to their marital status, much to the delight of the soccer coaches. During the day it was high quality, intense soccer, fol-

"Still waters run deep" is an old statement that proved to be frighteningly true one night when the mother arrived back at their home. The husband grabbed the mother and forced her neck into a noose, pulling it tight. He then produced a loaded gun and pressed it against his wife's head, threatening to kill her. Seemingly he finally escaped and went missing. He was finally found by the police, prosecuted, and I believe spent time in rehab. I felt great empathy for the man's situation, losing a wife, child, job, and carrying a criminal record for the rest of his life.

Despite this incredible story of a near murder, many of the mothers continued to fall for the accents of the British coaches who were also fit and athletic. Soccer in 1990 was a sport few, if any, of the dads or moms had played, so the pro coaches were held in unrealistic high esteem despite the fact that most of them made less than the parents' gardeners.

Living the American Dream

After nine years living in San Diego, Pauline and I were well settled into the relaxed lifestyle of Southern California. We had bought a beautiful, single level home on the border of Pacific Beach and La Jolla, only five minutes from the beach and Pacific Ocean. Pauline now had a full time teaching job earning good money, and with my soccer coaching money from the Nomads, soccer camps, and successful real estate career, we were financially prosperous. When we had emigrated from England almost ten years earlier, we had left behind a very comfortable lifestyle, including a beautiful house and upscale cars. Now we once again had the trappings of success with Pauline driving a new BMW 5 Series and my new 560 SL Mercedes sports convertible. We ate out regularly at nice restaurants in Pacific Beach and La Jolla and enjoyed our marriage, without the duties or responsibilities of any children of our own.

Often we were asked why we had never had children. Truthfully, we had only discussed it on a few occasions, and I was honest enough to admit that I was too selfish to burden myself with the demands of my own children. One night in a lovely restaurant, I was telling Pauline how much I enjoyed watching Bob's relationship with his son, TK. I was also reminiscing on the late Kurt Yokes and the joy his father derived from the relationship with his son. Pauline gently pointed out that Bob played basketball, performed in a band, was my team manager, and was a very wealthy, successful stockbroker. Having a son (and a beautiful daughter, Ashley) didn't stop Bob from leading a varied, exciting life of his own. Kurt's dad, Bob, had also been a successful businessman but found lots of time to be with his son and other children.

Strangely, after 20 years together without little more preamble, we left the restaurant, decided that we would try to have a family of our own. My one condition was that if we could not succeed, we would not get into tests, artificial means, or other medical tricks. All or nothing. We went home that night to practice and begin the process. We were high with euphoria. Leaving for the restaurant that evening, there had been no thought of children or family on either of our minds. Now we headed home, two married people close to 40 years of age, 20 years together, looking to the next phase of our lives together.

Another piece of the jigsaw was beginning to fall into place when the U.S. government adopted an amnesty policy for "illegal aliens" who had been in the country before 1983. I read the rules and regulations relating to the "amnesty" and realized that we could benefit from this huge opportunity. Because I had been "legal" since 1981, working under a number of H.I. visas I would not qualify as an "illegal alien." Ironically, my wife would be able to apply, since she had been working "illegally," despite having a valid social security card. Pauline was wary of moving forward with this once in a lifetime opportunity, fearing the Immigration Department and any reprisals. The deciding factor was that my H.I. working visas would soon expire and there was no way for us to obtain the coveted "Green Card" to become Permanent Residents of the U.S. In coaching I had proven adept at receiving yellow cards and red cards over the past years, but this attempt at a "Green Card" legislation was crucial.

One evening we arranged to meet at the Amnesty Center in Mission Valley, to hopefully begin the process. We arrived in separate cars both dressed immaculately. When we entered the offices, the government officials looked at us as if we were from the Pentagon!

"Can I help you two?" a serious-looking agent inquired cautiously.

"Yes," I replied. "We are here for amnesty."

"You are not serious. This amnesty is not for people like you," he said in a somewhat confused state.

"My wife qualifies. We have been here since 1981 and we want to apply for amnesty and ultimately receive Legal Resident Status," I said politely.

It was a long, laborious process, but two years later Pauline received her Green Card and became a Legal Resident of the USA. Perversely, I then had to apply as her Dependent Husband and finally acquired the precious Green Card – in the nick of time!

It was meant to be. Within a few weeks of her coming off the pill, I was stunned to receive the news that my wife was pregnant! When the shock wore off, the excitement set in. Then, as was normal with my clever, organized wife, we needed to pay attention to details. Would she continue to work? If so, how many days? Who would help with the baby while she was at work? We signed up for Lamaze classes with a disbelieving nurse who thought we were the grandparents to be. A portent of things to come? Pauline's pregnancy went smoothly, and she continued to work out at the gym and keep in good shape while working full time at her teaching job. Would we have a son who would become a great soccer player – oops! The beginnings of a desperate soccer dad?

I had pointed out that as a teacher she actually only spent about 190 days a year in school. With her school necessitating about two hours for the roundtrip each day, going part time didn't make sense. We decided that she would take maternity leave, and when that was over, we would hire a live in nanny.

For some reason, we decided to advertise in England,

using Pauline's sister, Susan, to oversee the advertising and interview process. The main part of the ad emphasized "A warm, sunny climate year round." We were inundated with applications! Susan picked out what she thought were the best six and forwarded them on to us. Having dinner together at home, Pauline pushed the six applications across the table and suggested that one lady clearly stood out above the others. I quickly scanned all six and agreed that the one my wife liked was also my choice. In her mid-forties with two college age children, she was divorced from a successful accountant in the upscale area of Bramhall. Elaine had grown up in a nice area of Manchester and was an avid tennis player and soccer fan. Her father had been a medical doctor and her educational background was impressive. Susan interviewed Elaine in England, was equally impressed, and the Illingworths had a nanny!

Pauline entered the final days of her pregnancy still working at school and working out in the gym. One morning she told me that she felt that it was happening so she would hurry to school, leave prepared work for her students, and meet me at the hospital. In view of the long distance to her school, I overruled her and drove her straight to the hospital. Despite our numerous Lamaze classes, several hours of labor and pain eventually necessitated the use of drugs. I waited anxiously next to the bed, watching in horror as the doctors tried to prise the baby out with terrifying use of forceps. Finally the C Section team was summoned and the doctor decided to try one more time with the forceps before handing over. With what seemed criminal force, a final tug, and suddenly a strange "object" started to appear. Our son, Daniel Lee Illingworth had arrived!!!

I still remember to this day the feeling of watching a

miracle at the birth of a human being. Squeamish by nature, I thanked God that I had witnessed this joy of nature. A son! A great soccer player and athlete, I hoped. Pauline and Danny soon were ready to come home and we traveled back to our home together as a family.

I tried to imagine what kind of dad I would become when my son (hopefully) began to play sports (soccer in particular) and I was the involved parent on the sideline. Maybe I would finally begin to understand what drove those Desperate soccer moms and dads to behave the way they did. Maybe I would be quick to criticize the coach of my son, or blame the referee for causing my son's team to lose the game.

I doubted it, as I looked at my beautiful, "perfect" son who I had no doubt would become a great athlete and incredible soccer player. No!!! I would not become the self-opinionated, narrow-minded desperate soccer dad – yet!

I was also learning about the joys and smells of my son's shin guards and socks when driving him home after a game!

Trouble Brewing at the Nomads – The End is Nigh!

The Dallas Cup victory received tremendous publicity for the team and me when we arrived back in San Diego. The Soccer America National magazine produced an article. "Nomads win Dallas Cup in Style!" The article went on to say how my side had played with an open, entertaining style, unlike many other Nomads teams. I didn't know the reporter or have any input in the article, but enjoyed the positive press coverage. Colin was also earning a huge following of parents and players within the Club and improving steadily as a coach. His Achilles heel was his outburst of overly aggressive behavior. He was now single and carefree. Derek viewed both of us with a mixture of disdain, admiration, disbelief and concern.

After we arrived back from The Dallas Cup, we went on a strict training regiment to get into shape, running six miles a day over a tough, hilly course in Clairemont. I often joined him, slogging up the hill at Tecolote Canyon, fighting our way up the steep Balboa Avenue incline. By the time the new season began, we were both in great shape.

During a pre-season tournament, both of us were enjoying success with our individual teams, and I turned up to watch his semi-final. A tough game was guaranteed, playing against a Celtic team that was one of the best in California. Playing on a narrow field, Colin worked on using the long throw in. It worked and his team scored, took the lead and held on valiantly until a few seconds before half-time. The Celtics played a through ball behind Colin's defenders. His goalkeeper advanced quickly off his line, but hesitated at the last second, allowing their forward to arrive first and flick the ball into the goal. Not the end of the world – tied game at half-time.

Colin had done a magnificent job organizing his team to perform so well against a superb opponent. He was bitterly disappointed to give up a goal on the stroke of hard time. Especially one that his goalkeeper should have dealt with. Unfortunately, his passion and disappointment got the better of him; something I and many other coaches have succumbed to. Without meaning to, his raised voice and body language were sincere but the perception, from a distance was negative. Still gaining experience in youth soccer coaching and the American attitude to kids and discipline, Colin genuinely tried to raise his team for the second half. Unfortunately, they lost to a more talented team.

The parents of Colin's goalkeeper sent a written complaint to the Nomads Board who convened on the following Thursday to consider it. Both myself and Colin were incredulous that for all his commitment to his team, one short incident could overrule all his great work. Fortunately, several of the Nomads Board of Directors were great admirers of his and good sense prevailed.

Colin was dedicated and anxious to improve and progress.

"Jeff, I have learned from this incident, and I will never make that mistake again," He didn't.

Nonetheless, our time at the Nomads was coming to an end since we both had our own views, disagreed with much of Derek's philosophies, and spoke our minds too often.

I was really upset when I was told that Jovan was being moved off my team to play up a year for the Nomads older team. The team was nowhere as good as mine and I genuinely felt that it was also not in the best interest of Jovan. I made my feelings known very loudly and clearly on many occasions.

At one of the coaches meetings after Derek had been

gone in England for eight weeks, Derek criticized the staff for not working diligently or with any commitment. Both Colin and I pointed out that we had won our leagues and were on a roll with our teams. We also pointed out that it was fascinating to know how Derek knew so much when he had been on vacation for two month in England. Derek obviously did not take kindly to the aggressive opposition to his leadership. He had a right to run the Nomads Club the way he wanted to, and if we didn't like it, we had a choice. Leave.

Early the next season, I was still fuming over the Jovan situation and told several parents in frustration that I was going to leave. The word obviously got back to Derek because one evening, eating dinner with Pauline and my best mate from England, Tony, and his wife Christine, I received a call. It was from Brian, Derek's assistant, friend, and partner telling me that they had heard of my desire to resign so they had accepted it and wished me well. I was speechless as he hung up the phone. When I arrived back at the dinner table, the other three people looked at me with concern. "I've just been fired from the Nomads! Let's celebrate!" I said with false enthusiasm.

Fortunately, over the previous few months I had talked several times in passing to Board members at the Surf Soccer Club and knew their Head Coach well.

When word got out that I was no longer at the Nomads, I soon had a meeting with the Surf, and we agreed that I would join their staff. Unfortunately, being part way into the season, there were no coaching vacancies available right then. I suggested that I referee for the remainder of the season so I could get to know the coaches, parents and players. One of the first people I had met at the Surf Club was the President, Mike Connerley. In my 28 years of coaching, Mike is still to me the shining example of what a soccer organizer and leader should be. I will talk more about Mike when I discuss his Tournament, The Surf Cup - in my opinion the Best Tournament in America!

A Bible For Parents – If You"re Not Sure, Say Nothing!

Both Colin and I had refereed many high school games together earning some extra "beer money" and having a good time doing it. We were both disdainful of the vast majority of the American referees who had officiated our games. We tended to referee in a pretty relaxed, laid back manner, trying to allow the players latitude to enjoy the game and express themselves. The never ending spate of "red cards" given to undeserving players was anathema to us both. If a player was becoming a real, ongoing nuisance, we would simply tell the coach to replace him with another player or else!

During one local game at Mission Bay High School, a visiting player went crazy and called me a "blind English moron." Colin was on the other side of the field, near to the opposing bench. Leaning toward the visiting coach, he calmly said, "Your player's absolutely right. I agree with him. However, he will have to leave the field and you can replace him without penalty." Nice job Colin.

On another occasion, I decided to give a rare yellow card. As the player stood in front of me, I fumbled in the pockets of my referee shirt. I hadn't brought any cards! Colin was on the other side of the field. I shouted across and asked if he had a yellow card in his pocket. The puzzled player stood there as Colin produced a battered looking piece of card resembling the color yellow. "See, you have been yellow carded," I said barely able to keep my face straight.

In another high school game at Mission Bay, a situation occurred that would have done Laurel and Hardy proud.

I arrived at the school, in my referee's uniform, only to discover that I had forgotten my soccer cleats. Several of the high school team played for Mission Bay Soccer Club, so I finally borrowed a spare pair of cleats from Brent, one of our players who kindly offered.

During the game, which was a tense play-off battle, with both sets of parents screaming consistently throughout. With the game tied, Brent attempted to clear the ball, but unfortunately for him, the ball sliced off his foot and flew into his own goal! There was a short, stunned silence, before the other side went crazy celebrating their good fortune. Brent stood forlornly, head down, shoulders hanging. One of the opponents started to taunt Brent, and before I could deal with it, Brent, out of frustration, gave him a smack. The opposing coach, players, and parents screamed for a red card, which was the only option.

Reluctantly I told Brent that he was red-carded and would have to leave the field.

Totally distraught, with tears in his eyes, this 17 year old young man turned to me and said,

"Not until you give me my cleats back!!!" (I am not making this story up – honestly!) The thought of taking off the cleats, giving them to a player I had just red-carded and then having to referee in stocking-feet, seemed beyond farcical. Finally I managed to gently persuade Brent that I was not angry with him and I had no intention of reporting him to the Soccer Trial Board. Finally he trudged off the field as I surreptitiously looked across the field to my referee partner who could barely contain himself from falling apart laughing.

My refereeing at the Surf Club for several months was to be an enlightening experience, and I am glad to this day I had the opportunity to "be on the other side of the fence." I took the refereeing challenge seriously, especially as I was given many of the Surf's top, elite, older teams to referee. Considering my infamous reputation for "verbal involvement" with referees when I was coaching, I decided to introduce my own method when I was the referee. I would bring both coaches to the center, introduce myself and inform them that I was committed to doing the very best job I could. Being realistic, I knew there would be calls they would not like, and I had no problem with them questioning the calls in a reasonable manner. I insisted, however, that I would not allow any parental dissent whatsoever from any sideline. I would hold the two coaches fully responsible for the behavior of all their parents. In some games the coaches knew me, were surprised to see me refereeing, and often had a laugh and a joke. Some former coaching opponents from battles in the past were less friendly.

The days were long and tiring, and I learned great respect for the physical demands of the job. My determination to exclude the parents from continually shouting out their opinions was based on one simple premise. They were wrong more often than not and were a pain in the ass! In 2008, I believe even more this to be the case. Even if you have played the game all your life, soccer is a difficult game to understand as the game unfolds. Ignorance of the obvious rules is bound to occur. Understanding the nuances of the game is impossible without real, in depth, unbiased knowledge of this fantastic, constantly in motion game.

Hundreds of times over the 28 years, I have been embarrassed by the ignorant behavior of both parents of my own players and the opposing players. There are regular, weekly errors of judgments I see continually. Here are a few examples:

1. Player throws the ball forward to an attacker who is in the opponent's penalty area. Parent shouts "offside ref." Wrong! You can't be offside from a throw in.

2. Attacking player dribbles past several defenders,

runs toward the goalkeeper and scores. Parents shout "Offside ref!" Wrong. The ball has not been passed to a teammate so no offside can occur.

3.   Player goes in to win the ball with a strong, aggressive tackle, getting the ball first and then causes the opponent to fall down. Parents shout "Foul ref. Yellow Card!" Wrong – just because a player gets tackled and falls down does not mean a foul occurred. Also, parents shouldn't be telling the referee to yellow card the other team. It is poor sportsmanship and is often incendiary, angering the opposing parents.

4.   A pass is played beyond the defense, and the attacker times his turn going past opponents, receiving the ball in space behind the defense. The parents of the defenders scream for "Offside!" Wrong – offside is judged where the attacking player was at the moment the ball was played, not where he is when he receives the ball. This particular situation is almost an "optical illusion." It happens so quickly that even at top professional levels, the linesman (assistant referee) get this wrong sometimes.

5.   A player fouls an opponent, the ball runs favorably for the attacking team, and the referee doesn't blow his whistle. Usually the parents go crazy, demanding a foul. Wrong – the referee has employed the "advantage rule" enabling the attacking team to continue on for their advantage. I only see this used by a few top quality referees. When it occurs, the parents of the "fouled" player never understand or accept the decision.

6.   A defender tries to clear the ball but miss kicks it and it spins backward to his goalkeeper, who picks it up. Parents shout that there should be a free kick because it was a back pass. Wrong – it was not a deliberate back pass; therefore, the goalkeeper has a right to pick it up. What actually happens is most young goalkeepers tend to not

pick it up being unaware or uncomfortable with the situation. I actually witnessed a situation as Head Coach, watching one of my coaches with his team, in a tournament final; lose to a penalty awarded to the opponents for a back pass. The decision was wrong in the first place because it was not a deliberate pass back to the goalkeeper. The young referee then compounded the mistake by awarding a penalty-kick instead of an indirect-kick. They scored and that was the "winning goal." We lodged a complaint about the penalty award (not the back pass). The poor referee was in tears when he realized his mistake. The Tournament Committee awarded "winners medals" to both sides. Refereeing is a tough job – mistakes happen.

7. A vast majority of the time, many parents on the losing team blame the referee for the results. One game, my team won 8-0 and the parents of the losing team confronted the referee for his poor performance! Where was their coach during their training sessions?

8. Parents who feel they are contributing to their team by screaming such banal phrases as "Go!" "Go get them!" "Run!" "Energy!" "It's our game!" are wasting their breath.

9. Standing on the sideline, coaching your own child is a waste of time. Trying to coach other players on your child's team is inappropriate, presumptuous, and can lead to real trouble, especially if you are saying negative comments to someone else's child. I had an incident last year where two of my fathers, unbeknownst to me, almost had a fist fight because one objected to the other commenting negatively on his daughter. Don't bother. Leave it to most of us English coaches. We will give enough negative criticism to our players without any help from parents!

Playing Time – A Guaranteed Source of Discord

Parents, who are unhappy with their own child's playing time, may try to enlist support from parents of other players who also play limited minutes. "I can't believe the coach only plays your child for so few minutes every game. Your child is a strong player and deserves better." How does the listening parent respond to such patronizing garbage? Ideally his response would be, "Thanks for your opinions, but honestly, I think the coach is doing a great job and has my support." Unfortunately "misery loves company," and the parent gets dragged down into the pit saying, "Thanks. Yes, I am frustrated that my child doesn't play more and your child also deserves more time on the field."

This is how the parental "cancer" can start to spread and undermine the team. In competitive youth soccer, playing time is an ongoing problem that can never be satisfactorily cured. At the highest, most extreme scenario in Southern California, we sometimes have players traveling 250 miles each way and not playing any minutes on the field. The parents of the stronger players who start and play many minutes are obviously more inclined to be "happy campers." As a parent myself of two sons now aged 19 and 20, I have seen the dilemma from the other side. I have come to the absolute conclusion that there is not perfect answer or resolution.

The simple fact is that if you can only have 11 players on the field and you have 16 players on your roster, five players have to be sitting on the bench. If you are a fortunate coach who has 16 players of similar ability, then substituting, particularly in big games, is not a major problem. However, in reality most all team squads have some players who are not as strong as the majority of the starting 11.

As a coach for almost 40 years, I am always cognizant of the feelings of the boy or girl, who is sitting on the bench, especially for a long time and in many games. However, I also have a professional obligation to the majority of the stronger players and their parents. Many years ago I substituted three players at a crucial time in an important game. Unfortunately, within six minutes, each of these players made vital errors, and from a 2-1 lead, we were 4-2 down. By the time I put the three starters back on the field, we could only pull back one goal and lost 4-3. Another type of loss came quickly. The three starting players I had brought off left my team to join one of our competitors who were "committed to winning if at all possible." Their parents were Desperate to win and would not accept substituting just for the sake of it. A lesson learned for me.

An argument that never ends and is rooted in the problem of playing time is the number of players on a roster. For an eight a side team, the maximum roster size is 14. Carrying this number is good for the budget, but bad for team harmony. In 11 a side, the roster can include up to 18 players – same problem! Parents are like a time bomb on the sideline looking at their child sitting forlornly on the bench.

"Hell hath no fury like a woman (mother) scorned."

After try outs, many clubs aim for 12 players on the roster on an eight a side team, and 16 players on an 11 a side team. Then comes the future problem of what to do over the ensuing months when new players move into the area, especially in the summer months. If a gifted, "star" player arrives on your doorstep, you don't sign them, they go to one of your competing clubs and you may never get a chance to have them in your team again. A moral and practical dilemma. For the newly arrived child, why should they be penalized for moving into the neighborhood after try outs - especially when try outs in San Diego are four or five months before the season begins? If you don't select 12 or 16 players and you don't get any late "star" arrivals, your budget is impacted, and should injuries occur or children move out of the area, your roster can be decimated.

During a tense semi-final with one of my boys" teams, I was continually imploring one of my forwards to move off the ball to create space for himself. Exasperated by my player who had blazing physical speed but a very slow thought process, I prepared to bring him off the field after only six or seven minutes. Suddenly I hear, "Will you leave my fu..iing son alone. You are always shouting at him!!!" A Desperate Dad. "Ref. Sub please." I took the boy off without looking behind me at the boy's dad. With dozens of parents and children on the sidelines, his profanity was ill-timed and unacceptable. He phoned the next day to apologize and we met to "clear the air." We were never going to resolve our differences. The dad thought his son was an "impact" player on our team, and I considered the boy a sort of unfulfilled talent on the soccer field. At the end of the season, the father moved his son to our nearest rivals, where he became a bench player for his new team!

Another unpleasant incident occurred on the field while I was coaching in my final year at the Nomads. During my first year, I had a U/16 boy's team with a very talented goalkeeper and a back up goalkeeper of modest talent. The back-up goalkeeper was a great young man with a forceful father who was governed by an even more dominant wife. I "inherited" the team from another coach with the two goalkeeper situation already in place. In the easier games, I tried to get my back up goalkeeper on the field as often as possible. In the big games, I could not get him any playing time, much to the chagrin of his parents. Eventually he moved on and I wished him well. Several years later I was watching a tournament game when I heard a rather unpleasant voice behind me. "I don't believe it! He's not still involved in coaching kids!" The parents of my former back-up goalkeeper were staring malevolently into my eyes. Trying to be humorous, I replied,

"Yes, I'm younger than I look." The humor fell on stony ground.

"You ruined our son's soccer career, you English piece of shit," the mother suggested forcefully.

"Yes, you bastard. He will never be the same again," segued the father, dutifully supporting his wife.

Considering this was a Thanksgiving tournament, their sentiments did not seem to fit with the mood of the holiday. I was reeling, due to the unexpected attack and the vitriol of these two parents. When I finally began to recover my composure, I was not happy with the verbal assault. In fact, the father was pointing his finger at me and offering threatening body language. Remembering my altercation a few years earlier on the same field in the same tournament, I sensed the threat of a physical altercation. Wisely, I started to walk way until I heard, "You see. He's a coward!" the father hissed. Now I was turning back toward him.

"Ask your wife to leave and meet me at the back of the hut. I'll be waiting for you," I suggested. High noon in La Jolla! Would I never learn? Fortunately, the threat took the bravado away from the father and he flounced away with his wife without saying another word. Unbelievable! We are talking about kids' soccer.

Moving forward 17 years to 2008, I was sitting at

Starbucks with my new wife, Robin, when a good looking man in his early thirties came up to us. "Hi coach! How are you?" asked my former back-up goalie, son of Satan and wife, also now a prominent broadcaster on a Soccer Channel. I had seen him several times on TV and was delighted to introduce him to my wife.

"I am delighted you are doing so well on TV. You are doing a great job," I complimented him.

"I am honored to see my favorite coach again. Although I wasn't a great goalkeeper, you stuck with me, treated me great, and always made me laugh," he replied. I wondered if he knew about the unpleasant scene I had with his parents many years ago. It seemed pointless to ask. His soccer career obviously had not been "ruined."

"I realized that I loved the game of soccer but wasn't a great player, so I began to look for other ways of staying involved in this great game. Your encouragement meant a lot to me," he said.

"And your words mean a heck of a lot to me," I thanked him as we shook hands and he left. My wife, not knowing what had transpired years before, realized there was some undercurrent and I explained the background to her.

Try-Outs and "Cutting Players" – The Heartbreak

So far I have dealt primarily with competitive youth soccer, as that has been my main area of coaching in San Diego for almost 30 years.

The worse part of the season is when try-outs roll around, which in San Diego is early in the year. As competition gets more and more fierce, try-outs get earlier and earlier – some in January for the younger ages. No matter the club, every try out brings successes, signing good new players, and the disappointment of losing good players, especially if the lost player comes as a shock to the coach.

By far, the worst coaching task is having to cut a player from your team who has become a great team member. Through no fault of their own, nor their great parents, the time has arrived where the team's progress necessitates replacing them on the roster. Real life as it may be, telling the parents and a young child that they are no longer on the team is a source of nightmares for any involved coach. Adding to the difficulty is when that player has siblings in the same club. This delicate, emotional dilemma can blow up in the face of a coach and the club. If one of the siblings is a high quality player, it may result in the parents pulling all their children out of the club. Over the last twenty years, the intense recruitment of the highest quality players has turned into a feeding frenzy in Southern California. Players as young as five years of age are now sought out and recruited by many top competitive youth soccer programs – including mine!

The really top youth soccer programs tend to be very businesslike, and when a new, better player is found, the expendable player is either relegated to a lower team or needs to find a new club. There is something very sad about the process when youngsters are on the "scrap heap" at 11 or 12 years of age or younger!

Informing the player and parents is a very delicate, sensitive task. When one of my coaches told me they had left a message on the family's recording machine, I knew the worst was to come. Sure enough, the youngster himself played the message first. When the parents heard their son crying and discovered the reason, I received one very angry phone call.

Improving competitive youth soccer teams is vital and necessary. Unfortunately, it may necessitate moving nice kids off the team.

The Cesarean Birth of a Soccer Nation

In the early 1980's, the fledgling youth soccer programs were often being introduced to American society by expatriates from Europe and South America. Fathers who had grown up with soccer in their home countries, or even grandfathers taking the trouble to organize and train a group of youngsters to play "competitive soccer" in a country where baseball, basketball and American football dominated, soccer faced seemingly insurmountable odds. Slowly, inexorably, soccer began to catch on in the 1980's with more and more children starting to play at an early age. Not only was the sport catching hold, but the incredible interest in soccer from a huge number of girls gave the sport an incredible boost. In fact, girls' participation in soccer was so profound, the USA soon became the Mecca for female soccer in the world.

Leagues started to appear everywhere, as well as an increasing number of tournaments all over California. The level of play started to increase rapidly as the vast numbers of young soccer players produced an increasing group of talented players. With the level of competition increasing, the need for quality coaching became a necessity, and starting with the Nomads, then Mission Bay Soccer Club, and the Hotspurs, suddenly all the ambitious competitive clubs were boasting professional coaches. A new profession had arrived in Southern California for sure. Nowhere in the world, to my knowledge, were there hundreds of paid soccer coaches working regularly with young amateur soccer players.

In its infancy, US soccer had created a new way of developing the world's biggest sport. I watched in awe as the game of soccer came to include almost every five and six year old child in San Diego. Fields appeared everywhere with hundreds of American youngsters playing this cute "new" game. Many pioneers like Joe Hollow at the Nomads, Jeff Bishop at the Villa Club, and Hank at Mission Bay unselfishly dedicated their own time, effort, and money to drive soccer forward. Mike Connerley at the Surf Club was building a tournament that was to grow into a world renowned event of the very highest quality. Mike Hovenic cleverly and efficiently developed a series of well run soccer camps around San Diego County. In other areas of the State and the USA, other volunteers and soccer experts were quickly and efficiently putting together recreational youth soccer and college programs. Ironically, when I returned each year to England, I was continually asked the same question – "When will soccer (football) catch on in the USA?" Even in 2009, the rest of the world still has no idea of the vast numbers of players – boys, girls and adults – playing soccer in the USA.

Simply because the US still has its three high profile pro sports controlling all the big advertising money, the professional soccer league, MLS, is still dwarfed by its competition – baseball, NFL football, and basketball. In its own inimitable way, the USA has created a magnificent soccer model, crafted in its image and design. It works! We have many US players playing in pro leagues all over the world, including a good number in the English Premier League.

On the other side of the argument is a large group of Americans who are dissatisfied, asking "Why can't we win the World Cup?" The simple answer is no country in the world can win the World Cup every four years except one - one country out of the dozens of countries who covet the biggest team prize in World Sports. As an example, England has only once won the World Cup in almost a hundred years. Unlike American sports where the "World Series" is only competed for within America by only

American teams, the soccer World Cup includes every country in the world, from the super powers of Brazil, Italy, France, Argentina, Germany and England, down to the Faro Island, Maldives, and other tiny outposts.

It is incredible how well the USA has done for a country so new to the soccer scene. Playing against its nearest neighbor and rival, Mexico, a fervent soccer nation, the US has dominated the recent games both at home and away. Also, in every other country in the world, success is the main game and all the best athletes are involved. In the USA, the lack of fame and huge money as that received in the big three sports, entices many great players to move away from soccer in their teen years.

Watching many TV ads on US television, it is incredible to see how many include a soccer ball or youngsters playing soccer. In the upscale neighborhoods I live in such as Carmel Valley and Del Mar in San Diego, there are 5,000 boys and girls playing soccer at either recreational or competitive levels. There are hundreds of top quality, well organized tournaments everywhere in Southern California throughout the year. My favorite is the Surf Cup in Del Mar, San Diego.

It should be noted that in basketball, golf, and baseball, American athletes no longer dominate with ease, with other emerging countries around the world improving rapidly. In 1950, America beat England in a World Cup game in Brazil. It was and still is, the greatest upset in World Soccer history.

For the current USA men's team to beat England, or any other top world team, would no longer be cause for shock tremors throughout the soccer world. We, in the USA are quickly earning the respect of the world's soccer community. Thanks to the success of our huge, well organized youth soccer programs and huge support of millions of dedicated soccer parents and kids.

The Surf Cup – Sun, Sand, Star Players

Over the 28 years I have lived and coached in San Diego, I have had the pleasure to be involved in many tournaments in California, Nevada, Arizona, and Texas. As I wrote earlier, the Dallas Cup is certainly one that has a worldwide reputation, especially with its Under 19 Super Group. However, for me, the tournament that has it all is the Surf Cup, held every summer in Del Mar, San Diego – not because it is near my house – honestly!

Envision 20 perfect soccer fields, side by side, under a clear blue sky, to "weather" with a cooling breeze from the nearby Pacific Ocean, superbly organized, with a huge scoreboard, continuously being updated throughout each hour of each day, twenty mouth watering field concession stands, and an enormous Nike tent selling every soccer product this industry giant produces. Oh yes, what about the quality of soccer!?

The first weekend is boys and girls Under 10 through Under 15 played the last weekend in July. The boys and girls U/16 – U/19 is played the first weekend in August. The venue is the exquisite fields of The San Diego Polo Club, ten minutes east from the shimmering sand of the beaches of Del Mar. Each weekend 25,000 – 28,000 people converge on this breathtaking event, much to the annoyance of the ultra wealthy residents of nearby Rancho Santa Fe.

Gaining admission to play in this great tournament is a challenge in itself which caters to only "THE BEST OF THE BEST." Reaching your State Cup semi-final or better in California insures a "guaranteed acceptance", which is no easy feat playing in Southern California, competing against many other high quality teams. Failing to qualify through this method, teams must submit their results and successes for the past year's games. A selection committee carefully examines and vets each application, searching to put together a tournament of only elite boys and girls teams at every age level. In the older age groups, the number of teams from outside the State and internationally increases exponentially. Over my many years, I have had the pleasure of seeing many teams from Britain, Hungary, Japan, Mexico, Sweden, and many other countries playing in the Surf Cup.

During the 1980's and early 1990's, Salford Boys City Team used to regularly play in the Surf Cup. This was my old team, selected from Salford, a huge city the size of San Diego, in England. They selected the best 18 players from all the schools in Salford to produce their "Town Team." Acknowledged in England as a top City Select Team, Salford was surprised to come all the way to The Polo Fields, only to leave the Surf Cup each year empty handed, often failing or struggling to get out of their group. I was intrigued to see USA "Club" teams giving the supervised English inner city tough youngsters a very difficult time.

One year, the Salford Team fought its way to the final, and ironically faced a team from Ireland. I had watched the Irish team play several times in the tournament and noted their best player, a dynamic forward with searing speed and a goal scoring knack. On the Saturday before the final, one of the Surf parents kindly offered the Salford Team a pool party at her beautiful home in Mission Hills, overlooking Balboa Park and Downtown. The combination of great food, a sparkling pool, suntanned young California girls in skimpy swim suits, and lots of alcohol at the party, was a recipe for disaster with these street smart, tough kids from Salford. As the night wore on, many of the English boys started disappearing into the huge house, as did a lot of the alcohol. The young American girls fell in love with the boys' accents and started to "pair up" romantically. Then, inevitably, the smell of cigarette smoke started to permeate the pool area. I felt uncomfortable and asked the Salford coaches to take control of the rapidly deteriorating situation.

Most professional soccer athletes spend the night before a big game relaxing, eating sensibly, no alcohol or lovemaking (well, maybe I'm pushing it a bit far!?). These 14 and 15 year old Salford boys, after four games played in heat that was foreign to them, were now in full "party mode." Several of the American parents stood with their mouths open as these young English visitors drank, smoked, and groped their daughters in preparation for the next day's semi-final at The Surf Cup. Having lived in San Diego for ten years since departing my school teaching job in Salford and Head Coaching position for an earlier Salford Town team, I had extreme mixed feelings. I felt embarrassment for the lovely lady who had kindly offered her hospitality to the Salford Team, pity for these young boys who knew no better since back home this kind of behavior was commonplace, and frustration and anger that the coaches in charge (friends of mine) had not stopped this behavior in its infancy.

I decided enough was enough and encouraged the players to get ready to depart in preparation for the "long, hard day" that faced them the following day. Very reluctantly, like dragging a dog away from a bone, the young men put down their now empty beer bottles, discarded their cigarettes, and tore themselves away from the exotic, nubile "California Babes."

Next day, showing their working class strength of recovery, they fought and clawed their way to a narrow win in the Surf Cup semi-final under a hot sun.

Their final was in the mid-afternoon, the hottest part of the day, facing a confident team from Ireland, boasting the MVP of the whole tournament – David Healey. Credit must be given to the Salford boys who fought for every ball, tackled ferociously, and showed their hunger and appetite for a fight. The game was tied at the end of full time, agonizingly taking the Salford boys into overtime of 30 minutes. This was the sixth game for both teams in only three days, playing on huge, full sized fields, against top quality opposition! Who can guess if the previous evening's indiscretions inhibited the Salford boys' chances? As I watched them toil under the hot California sun, white skin burning and turning redder by the minute, I felt great empathy for these Salford boys. Having taught in Salford for six years, I was very cognizant of their tough, socially deprived backgrounds. Here they were in one of the world's wealthiest, most beautiful areas, toiling valiantly to succeed. Late in overtime, the talent and speed of the Irish forward, Healey, proved too much and Salford finally succumbed. Nobody watching could avoid feeling an affinity for the vanquished English boys.

I have followed the progress of David Healey since that Surf Cup, and he has proved my estimation of him to have been correct. After several years at Manchester United, he is now playing for Sunderland in the English Premier. He is also a prolific goal scorer for his Irish National Team.

Healey is one of many great youth players who have graced the Surf Cup, before going on to successful college and pro careers.

Sadly, over the years the Salford Team has stopped participating in the Surf Cup, which I find an indictment of their coaches' unwillingness to play against THE BEST OF THE BEST.

Bodyguards in the Surf Cup!

One of the most interesting teams to enter the Surf Cup was England's most famous private school - Eton. Home to Britain and the world's richest and most upper class families, Eton personifies England's penchant for elitism and the class system. The team they sent was nowhere near strong enough to compete in the top bracket of their age group so they were entered in the B bracket. One particular player of theirs was the talk of the tournament. He was the grandson of one of the richest oil princes in the Middle East. This young man was shadowed 24 hours a day by four armed bodyguards who looked exactly what they were – big, tough, unsmiling men dressed incongruously in suits and ties as they stood on each side of the field. As the young prince ran around the field, his four bodyguards positioned themselves to be able to view all the people around the field watching the game.

The scene had a surreal feel to it as an everyday event unfolded on a beautiful soccer field in a safe, upscale community, four highly trained bodyguards "surrounded" a kids soccer game. This is unfortunately a sign of the times. For the record, the Eton team was average, and the prince was fortunate that he had a good "day job" waiting for him back in his oil kingdom.

Surf Cup – The Perfect Soccer Vacation

Because of the difficulty of gaining acceptance to this prestigious tournament, only a privileged few young players are fortunate enough to participate in this great event. My advice to all soccer families is to come to San Diego for your family vacations at the same time as the Surf Cup is happening. I happily spend eight hours each of the three days wandering around the 20 fields enjoying watching the numerous quality games in progress throughout the day.

The Surf Club has one of the top girls' programs in the world, directly by my old mate, Colin. He has been head of the Surf program for more than 12 years and has done a magnificent job. He has truly matured into a great coach and a strong, dynamic leader of a nationally respected youth soccer program. The "Old Days" with me and him "The Odd Couple" seem a lifetime away.

The atmosphere for three days each of the two weekends is soccer "magic" as the strongest teams start to emerge from the groups. Exceptional players begin to stamp their authority in the games and long standing rivalries play out in dramatic fashion. With thousands of moms and dads, many who have traveled thousands of miles, the tension is extremely high. Teams who arrive with high hopes are quickly brought down to earth as they face quality opposition they have never experienced beforehand. Teams from Europe and South America naively unaware of the progress of soccer in the USA arrive expecting to "teach the Americans the game of soccer." Many return home with their tails between their legs.

In the middle of all this excitement, the Tournament Director, Mike Connerley, stands calmly next o the enormous scoreboards. After 28 years, he is the doyen of all tournament directors. Working the scoreboards expertly are his lovely wife, Sue, and Mikes longstanding friend and helper, Jamie Tuckey. Sadly, Mike's very close friend and right hand man, Mick Dawson, who contributed so much to the organization of the Surf Cup, recently passed away. The tournament will continue to commemorate this wonderful man.

Many spectators have no connection with any of the participating teams. They simply attend to take advantage of the opportunity to watch most of America's top soccer players competing on the finest "stage."

If you are reading this and want the best soccer watching family vacation available, plan to spend either three days at the younger Surf Cup or three days at the older (16-18) weekend. The older weekend attracts more than one hundred college coaches from all over the USA. Sitting for many hours, these coaches take advantage of watching, up close, hundreds of potential college recruits playing at the highest level.

For all clubs or coaches who aspire to run their own soccer tournament, my advice would be to come and experience the seamless organization of this great event. If everything in our USA youth soccer was run this way, everyone's soccer experience would be that much more positive.

I look forward to this year's 2009 Surf Cup and pray, as usual, that one or more of my own club's teams earns the right to be accepted. If not, I will be there enjoying my feast of soccer, watching THE BEST OF THE BEST.

A Second Son – Life is Perfect

Eighteen months after my son, Danny, was born, my wife Pauline presented us with another beautiful son, Benjamin James Illingworth. Two great sons, a wife and partner of more than twenty years, and thriving new life of ten years living in beautiful San Diego.

I had just celebrated my 40th birthday with Pauline organizing a surprise party that took me completely by surprise. After Colin and I had done our 40 minute torture run up and down Tecolote Canyon, Colin was in a generous mood, offering to buy me a couple of beers at Baxter's Bar in Clairemont. Every time I mentioned going home, he generously bought me another birthday beer. (I should have known something was going on!) Finally he agreed to drive me home. Arriving at my home in Pacific Beach, I unsuspectingly walked through the front door into the hushed living room and dozens of surprise guests waiting to celebrate my 40th birthday.

Life was as perfect as it could be – great wife, family, career, super health, training for a triathlon; I felt on top of the world. I was also enjoying my real estate career, which was producing good money and worked perfectly with my soccer coaching career.

A stroke of fortune had come my way when I was given a wonderful present for my newborn son by the parents on one of my teams. Sending a letter of thanks to them, I added on a mention of my real estate career should any of them have anything in real estate I could help them with. I had always demurred from handing out my real estate business cards so as not to put the parents in a difficult position or create a conflict of interest with my soccer coaching and my real estate careers. I actually felt a little uneasy about even writing about the real estate at the end of the thank you note. "Ask and thou shall receive."

A few weeks later, one of my player's mothers called me to say she and her husband knew all the top realtors in La Jolla. However, they had decided to use me as their realtor. They wanted to upgrade from their already beautiful house in La Jolla to what amounted to a mansion in La Jolla. The prospective house she mentioned was one that I often passed on my way to training with a tennis court, beautiful gardens, and a view of the Pacific Ocean. Soccer moms (and dads) had been a thorn in my side, pain in the ass, and even physically threatening over the past years. Here was another type of desperate mom! Desperate to buy a superb home in chic La Jolla and have me act as her real estate agent. I was also afforded the opportunity to sell their current home off La Jolla Mesa in a very nice neighborhood. The sum total of commissions I would receive on completion of these two transactions would equate to two years of soccer coaching, including summer camps. I couldn't believe my good fortune! A life lesson in "If you don't ask …." To make it even better, Molly and her husband, Ken, were elegant, classy people who treated me and others with great respect.

It was no difficult task to drive Molly around looking at elegant homes all over La Jolla. Their original choice had not been the right house, so the search was on while I also was working hard to sell their current home. I was to learn another life lesson – in real estate. "Buyers are liars." Even if they don't mean to be! Ken, the husband, had given me a clear list of the type of home they required:

1. Large, Spanish style
2. Room for large swimming pool
3. Great ocean views
4. Room for tennis court
5. Not in the lower Hermosa area of La Jolla – too near the La Jolla High School.

I was vigilant about keeping up with every house for sale that came available on the market in La Jolla. One Wednesday morning, I was on "caravan" viewing new listings on the market in La Jolla with other members of La Jolla REBA (Real Estate Brokers Association). One of the houses was a magnificent Spanish style house, completely rebuilt, like new, priced at $1,995,000. The house and the price range for my clients were perfect. However, the house had no room for a large pool, especially a tennis court, and no ocean view. The most important negative was the location – lower Hermosa, close to the high school. Pity, I thought "if only." But I was unwilling to mention the house and have Ken and Molly believe I was not listening to their wishes. The following Sunday, I left to run one of my Summer Camps in Fresno.

Midway through the week, I received a call from Molly saying that they had seen the "perfect house." She said, pleasantly, that she was surprised I had not seen it on last Wednesday's "caravan." "You don't mean Tom Groff's listing on Via Del Norte do you?" I asked incredulously.

"Yes! Yes! That beautiful Spanish home!" Molly replied excitedly. "Why didn't you mention it before you left town?" she asked.

"Molly, of all the things Ken listed for me to look for, almost none of his requirements for your new home fit Via Del Norte. There's no room for a pool or tennis court. No ocean view and it's in the heart of La Jolla Hermosa, an area Ken specifically said you guys did not want," I explained carefully and respectfully. Then came the Life Lesson in Real Estate!!! "But it's the Home of our Dreams!!!" Molly said, adoringly. Less than two months later, I had sold their home off La Jolla Mesa and we closed escrow a couple of days before Christmas on the "Dream House" in LOWER HERMOSA! My decision to leave the head coach job at El

Cajon Hotspurs had been well and truly justified. On Christmas Eve, I received a commission check equivalent to five years of salary at the Hotspurs. Thank you two great soccer parents!

Christmas the next day was a joyous celebration at the Illingworth household with two beautiful young sons opening their Christmas presents and two adoring parents giving praise and thanks for our good fortune.

Several weeks later I coached Ken and Molly's son in an important State Cup game. Due to circumstances and difficulty of the game, I only played their son for five or six minutes. Credit to them, despite all they had done for me and my family, they never complained or tried to make me feel I owed them a favor. DESPERATELY NICE PARENTS!

After a decade of living in San Diego and working extensively in youth soccer, several guiding principles had clearly emerged.

A. It was a wonderful job, coaching talented youngsters in the California sunshine.

B. The biggest problems and pressure comes from the parents.

C. Job security was not inherent in this limited career environment.

D. Competition for good players between the major youth soccer clubs was fierce and growing as each year passed.

E. The opportunity to earn big money for coaching youth soccer was extremely limited other than running your own soccer camps.

F. Within each Club was on ongoing power struggle between coaches/parents/board members/head coach. Because paid youth soccer coaching was in its infancy, there were no accepted pay scales, working conditions, contracts, or "game plan" of how to develop a youth soccer program.

New Club – The Surf – New Problems 1991 – 1995

Having fulfilled my refereeing commitments to the Surf Soccer Club, I now joined their coaching staff as previously agreed. Boasting magnificent fields, a superb tournament, many good teams, based in an extremely upper class neighborhood, the Surf Club was a classy club with an old friend, Malcolm, directing the coaching staff. Ironically, I had interviewed Malcolm many years earlier for the job of my assistant at Mission Bay Club. At that interview, I asked Malcolm what salary he was looking for. When he replied, "The same salary that you are being paid, Jeff," that was basically the end of the interview.

At the Surf Club there was a strong coaching staff of experienced coaches soon to include my old mate, Colin. Gary was a former successful pro-player from the top English league who had also been successful in the San Diego Sockers Pro Indoor team. He was now a member of the coaching staff of an easy going, likable, trustworthy, and hard working team. He had a regular day job driving a delivery truck in addition to coaching at the Surf. With small children at home, he had a very busy schedule but never complained. One of the high profile coaches and a close friend of Malcolm's was Henry, a tough looking Mexican. Henry was a free spirit who lived life to excess and was a "runaway train wreck" about to happen. A few years down the road, the whole of the Surf Club was to be rocked to its foundation by Henry's actions.

I settled in to a pleasant coaching schedule and enjoyed my three teams of young, under eight boys team, a good under 12 boys team, and a very strong under 16 boys team. I was also intrigued to watch several superb girls" teams training next to me. After all these years, I still had not coached a girls' team of my own. I was still not really in the loop of the enormous impact of girls' soccer in American society. One of the great rewards of coaching at the Surf was gaining a greater understanding of the incredible talent of the many girl players at the Surf. I little realized how the future would throw me head first into the joy, but differing demands, of coaching talented young ladies.

Malcolm was a hands off head coach who allowed his staff to coach in their own style as long as everything ran smoothly. Because the Surf Club entered many big tournaments, travel and hotels were an integral part of the coaching demands. Most of my players were local families, and I had few Hispanic players on my team or the club, unlike the Nomads Club.

I soon developed a great rapport and friendship with several parents in my under 12 boys' team who were all close friends with each other. It wasn't until I attended a party at one of their homes that I realized the wealth of that particular group of families. Low key, non controversial, and respectful to me, these successful people were from the village of Rancho Santa Fe, voted the best place to live in the United State.

My early months also introduced me to the after practice happy hour at an elegant bar across the street from the Polo Fields. This was Henry's domain where he "held court" with coaches, parents (mainly mothers from the Surf), and even some of the players along with their mothers. On the many road trips in nice hotels, Henry shared that he could "party" with the BEST OF THE BEST. He was a fun guy to be around, if somewhat dangerous.

The Surf was about to hire my mate Colin to join me and Henry. Colin had finally moved on from the Nomads. He was refereeing as many games as he could to earn money, but really wanted to get a coaching job.

Fortunately, I managed to get him a job at the Surf. The one difference with the three of us was that I was married and had two sons at home. My incredible life in the sun and soccer plus a great family was there for me. Only I could destroy it. AND I DID!

You're Not A Real Referee!

With me now committed to coaching at the Surf, it seemed that my refereeing career was over, or certainly on hold. I enjoyed watching the wide-variety of referees that officiated both my home games and when we played away. The enormous chasm from the very best to the worst was stunning to behold. Old, over-weight, bald men who could barely run but could provide a decent job of refereeing a game. Young boys and girls frantically trying to referee junior games or act as assistant-referees. Occasionally a lady referee in her 20's or 20's – often very capable – sometimes a little aggressive or defensive.

I arrived at one of the Surf games to watch at the end of the day, noting it was a young girls' game and I was interested to see the standard of play. With my games over for the day, I sat in a chair and relaxed, waiting for the game to commence. It became apparent that the delay starting the game was due to the lack of a referee or assistants. The game was between the team in second place in the League – the Surf – and their opponents, who were top of the League. With talk of the game being abandoned or forfeit, I walked over to the opposing coaches and offered to officiate the game for them. The opposing coach, a young lady in her early 20's, looked at me as though I had used a profanity.

"You're not a real referee!" she snorted dismissively.

I explained to her that in addition to an "A" Level English coaching license, an English Teaching Degree, and 17 years involved in youth soccer coaching, I also had a referee's qualification.

"Where's your referee uniform?" she demanded.

"I have been coaching all day so I had no need to bring my referee uniform. I was somewhat "miffed" that my generous offer to referee a U/10 game (for free) was being treated with such disdain.

Reluctantly, the opposing coach (after spelling out to me the enormous importance of the game) agreed to ALLOW ME to referee.

Unusually, the field was very wet and somewhat muddy as we began the game. I had borrowed a whistle, which was positioned precariously between my cold, wet fingers.

After only 10 minutes, a player from the opposing team shot a high, fierce drive toward the Surf goal. A diminutive Surf player threw her hands in the air to protect herself. It was Sods Law – the ball hit her hands full on and flew back out of the penalty area. As blatant a penalty decision as you would ever see. I quickly moved the whistle toward my mouth, to award a penalty kick. Unfortunately, the whistle flew out of my hand, hit the grass, and an onrushing player stepped on it. Meanwhile the opposing coach was screaming for a whistle and an obvious penalty kick. Frantically I was on the ground searching to find my whistle. Both sets of parents were at a loss as to why the referee was on his knees looking in the grass and mud. The opposing coach was now apoplectic with anger. I found the whistle! Unfortuantely, in the meantime, the Surf team had counter-attacked from the blatant "handball" and raced to the other end to score. If looks could have killed, I would have been buried on the spot – with my muddy whistle!

I jogged over to a confused, angry, screaming, pointing, belligerent (you get the picture) coach.

"What the hell do you think you are doing?" she bellowed. "What about our penalty? What were you doing scrambling on the field?"

Good questions! Trying to explain the loss of my whistle and unfortunate stamping lacked credibility, so I simply apologized and turned to go back to the half-way line to begin the game. Surf 1 – Opponents 0.

At half time after innumerable disdainful comments from the opposing coach ("I knew he would be crap") and the parents – "Has he any kind of mental issues?"

I spoke to the coach and apologized. "It was a freak accident." She shook her head and shrugged her shoulders as she walked way disgustedly.

Fortunately, they scored two in the second half – including a penalty kick I awarded them (genuinely!), with a loud blast of my whistle. They won and left happy ("happier"). What do you expect from a referee when it's free???

La Jolla Lazers 1992 – 1995

I was told by one of my normer Nomads team managers that the La Jolla Lazers program was in serious need of leadership and change of direction. I followed up on this suggestion and found that since their former director of coaching had been sent to prison for having sex with an underage girl, the organization had drifted aimlessly. With La Jolla being such a wealthy area, finding money to pay a head coach would not be a problem.

I was hired and given freedom to try and upgrade the program. Our home base was Allen Field which we shared with the Nomads, my former employer. Obviously, my former boss, Derek, was not happy having me under his nose sharing the same field. Even worse, I was also employed by his arch-enemy, the Surf Soccer Club. The upside was that Derek had no sway in the La Jolla Lazers organization. In fact, the Lazers had much more a right to use Allen Field which had been donated by a well known real estate gentlemen, Willis Allen, for the benefit of the La Jolla Community.

Derek and I were unlikely "bed-partners," and an uneasy peace existed as the months passed by. I started to get momentum going with the Lazers' program fairly quickly using the pent up demand in the community for competitive soccer but not of the Nomads variety. Starting with a small group of "loosely affiliated teams," I started to work with their volunteer coaches to upgrade the quality of these teams. It was a pleasant working environment away from The BIG TIME SPOTLIGHT of coaching for the elite clubs. Steadily recruiting, advertising, and promotions, the Lazers "under the radar" club started to grow from its infancy of only four teams. Great kids and superb fields overlooking the Pacific Ocean meant a great life The extra income from the Lazers, plus my salary from the Surf Club added up to a solid income supplemented by my real estate commissions.

Surf/Lazers – England Soccer Tour 1992 – Teenage Boys and Girls Spell Real Trouble!!!

With my jobs going well at the Surf and the Lazers, I managed to put together a group of 15 year old Lazers girls and sixteen year old Surf boys for another England soccer tour. Funnily, as I write this, it seems so obvious that this pairing of young ladies and young men together was asking for trouble.

As usual, I traveled to England several days before the group was to arrive so I could visit my family and friends in addition to finalizing arrangements for the tour. I also needed to meet the "host families" who had kindly agreed to house the boys and girls for the duration of our stay in the Manchester area.

I met the large group as they arrived early morning at Manchester International Airport. The group included several parents who had agreed to supervise the children on the long flights from San Diego, via Chicago, to Manchester. One look at several adults' faces told me it had not been a trouble free journey. The evidence was staring me in the face. Before meeting at San Diego Airport, none of the boys or girls had ever met each other. As they came through customers, they were holding hands, cuddling, and in some cases, had their arms wrapped around each other. I asked them all if they were comforting each other because they felt shy in a foreign country. That was the last time the word "shy" was used or displayed on the whole trip.

One of the parents who had flown in with the group explained shamefacedly that the experience had been somewhat close to an orgy. Two of the girls were sisters who did not play for the Lazers but were friends of one of the Lazers players on the tour. In hindsight, I am embarrassed to say that I had never met them before they landed in Manchester. Nor did I meet the mother! We communicated by phone in San Diego and she sent a check immediately by mail. One sister was 14 years old but looked 17, and the other was 16 but looked 20, and both were very attractive. I had never been known for my naiveté or lack of savoir-faire, but in this situation, I was truly asleep at the wheel.

For some reason, I forgot about my ill fated school trip that I organized in 1979 to London. I was teaching at Ordsall High School, Salford near Manchester. I directed a group of 25 boys and girls, with the help of three other teachers, on a four day sightseeing tour of London. These were street smart kids with lots of energy and very little fear who would never normally travel outside of their own city.

About 10:20 PM on the first night I asked my colleagues, Anne and Rene, to check on the girls who were now in their hotel rooms. Curfew was 10:00 PM. They were gone for a long time and my good mate and colleague, Mike, and I continued chatting and drinking our beer. Finally they returned somewhat agitated and shaking their heads. They told me that they had arrived at the girls' rooms in time to find them all wearing makeup and lipstick. Our young ladies were preparing to leave the hotel and enjoy themselves having a night on the town in swinging London. I repeat, they were 15 years old!

Half an hour later, I asked Rene and Anne to give the girls one more visit just in case. My premonition turned out to be horribly right. The girls were literally climbing out of the window of their hotel room, escaping into the night. They brought the girls to me, their dynamic leader. For once I was shocked. The girls looked like they were dressed for business, ready to sell their bodies, wearing mini-skirts, low cut blouses, and heavy makeup. I could barely recognize them. Recovering my composure, I realized the incredible risk involved should they "fly the coop" and disappear. Reluctantly I asked if Rene and Anne would be willing to sleep in the same rooms as the girls. Graciously they agreed.

I had made my mind up that I would send the girls home the next day by train. I immediately called one of the few parents who had a phone and informed him of our problem. The dad seemed somewhat under whelmed and even surprised that I was making such a big deal about it. "My daughter goes out every Friday and Saturday with her mates, dancing and having a few bevvies," the dad informed me. By now, I realized he had drunk a "few bevies" himself that very evening. I had checked the train times from London back to Manchester and informed the dad what time they would be arriving back at Piccadilly Station, Manchester. I did not warn the girls as I was worried that with nothing to lose, they may turn awkward and run out of the hotel anyway.

Next morning, I warned our coach driver of our change in plans, then gave the girls the "good news." "I regret to tell you ladies, but I can no longer take responsibility for you under these circumstances. I am sending you home by train." Rene, who was a great teacher and a great friend, had kindly agreed to accompany them back to Manchester as I didn't feel comfortable letting them travel alone. When they heard what was happening, one of the girls, Louise, showed her class and upbringing.

"You've got to be fu..ing joking!!! We did nothing wrong. It's not as though you found us in our room shagging men!" Reasoning and diplomacy were not appropriate and I simply stated,

"You're going back. End of story!" After a few minutes,

they reappeared with their clothes already packed. After a tense drive to Euston Station, Renee and our fuming "young ladies" departed and we headed off to see Buckingham Palace.

Several months later, the girl with the foul mouth, Louise, walked into the school secretary's office while I was on the phone. A few second later I saw her exiting the school gates walking across the street to a house opposite. I asked Jean, our secretary, why Louise had left school early. She explained that the girl felt sick and her grandmother lived across the street. After my incident in London with Louise, I felt that maybe Jean had been wrong to believe her story. It turned out that our secretary was very right and I was very wrong. The girl died that night from some undetected brain problem. Thankfully, I had not interfered in letting her leave school on medical grounds. Much as she was a challenge, I always liked Louise who reminded me in some ways of a female version of me as a youngster; truculent, outspoken, cocky, and energetic. It was a sickening end to a young life.

Meanwhile, 1992, back at the Manchester Airport. I greeted all our "young lovers" and the parents. I specifically introduced myself to the two sisters who I had never met before. They looked me up and down as if I was on a casting call or audition for a part in a movie. A small shiver ran through me. Fourteen days was a long time to keep all these hot-blooded teenagers busy and out of trouble. With everybody on the bus, our driver headed off with a full bus load to rendezvous with our host families. I surreptitiously took in the dynamics of my mixed group of teenagers and parents. Hormones were bouncing off all sides of the bus as we pulling into The Derby School in the town of Bury. For more than an hour, I worked matching my players with their host families as both sets of youngsters,

Americans and English, "got to know each other." I think the term "meat market" is apropos for what was taking place. Finally my young players were all gone to their host homes.

My friend, Steve, who taught at The Derby School and arranged the host families, invited Tom, one of my American parents, and me to go for a beer at the local pub. Tom was a quiet, conservative Assistant Bank Manager who was relishing the new experiences. The local pub was across the street in a lower working class area. We all entered The Vault, the men's only room, and Steve ordered the beers. Tom and I sat at an empty table near to the dart board which had four tough looking guys engrossed in a doubles match.

"Ah! Real England" purred a smiley Tom. Just then, one of the darts players shouted, "Fu..king Bast..d!" in deference to a poor shot he had made. Tom tried to hide his surprise. Steve arrived back with the beers and sat down with us as a ring of cigarette smoke started to envelope us. All four darts players were smoking, or more accurately, had cigarettes burning away in the ash trays at their table. Tom started to cough and blink his eyes rapidly. Yes, Tom, it was real England! Tom's discomfiture was complete when one of the darts players started to suffer a problem with flatulence. It was obvious that he felt no embarrassment with his "gas" problem as he filled the room with the sounds and smells of his digestive failings. I didn't know whether to laugh or cry as I discretely watched Tom's embarrassed, changing reactions to the uncouth display. Finally, for Tom's sake, we left the pub and headed for our hotel accommodations where the parents and I were staying.

The next day I rendezvoused with all my groups and we headed to the beautiful Cheshire Village of Prestbury, a classic English village. We spent three hours there enjoying the ancient churches and graveyards, peaceful, rippling streams, and discovering the "terrible two sisters." They were sitting confidently at a village pub bar together with two of my Surf players enjoying a relaxing beer each! Even in England, 14 year old girls are not normally welcome to help themselves to alcohol. Agitated and frustrated, I "kicked them out" of the pub with a stern warning about their future conduct. The pub landlord apologized profusely, arguing correctly that they all looked older than eighteen.

That evening we played our first soccer game with the Surf boys" team easily beating an ordinary Bury school team. The girls' game was an interesting contrast in cultures with my La Jolla girls team consisting of attractive, athletic young ladies. The English ladies team was mainly in their twenties and thirties, many of them somewhat masculine looking. If it had been a street fight, we would have been destroyed. I prayed that the other team didn't offer or provide communal shower facilities at the end of the game! We won the game. The English women lacked basic skills and were nowhere near as physically fit as my girls.

After the game, all my players were picked up safely by their host families and I happily drove to meet Steve at a delightful local restaurant. Relaxed and enjoying our food and wine, Steve and I chatted about our forthcoming summer camp work together in California. Steve had worked for me during the summer and had become a valuable member of my staff.

After a pleasant evening, I arrived back at my hotel where I had an urgent message waiting for me from one of my host families. Surprise, surprise – it was the family hosting the "sisters from hell." As I listened to the lady who was hosting these two girls explain heatedly how they had hastily disappeared out of her front door "dressed to the nines." She had no idea where they had gone or with whom they had met. Only THIRTEEN DAYS TO GO!

Next morning after receiving an early call that they had in fact arrived back eventually at their host home, I confronted the sisters. Sending children home from London to Manchester was difficult but realistic. Sending two promiscuous teenagers home on their own from Manchester, England to San Diego, California was fraught with danger. Nevertheless, I needed the threat of sending them home early, plus a call to their mother to give myself any chance of avoiding a disaster over the next one and a half weeks. The most I could achieve was to contain the situation to collateral damage.

The host mother finally gave up on her two recalcitrant American visitors when they started making advances on her husband. I was forced to move them, and thanks to Steve, we found them a family where the father of the house would stand no nonsense or flirtatious behavior.

Finally our stay in Manchester was over and we headed south for our three day stay at Royal Holloway College outside of London. (The College was the first all girls college in the world when it was founded decades before.) With the tour now within sight of the finish line, I was counting the hours to boarding the plane and heading back to the USA.

Moving the large group around the Center of London was a logistical challenge so we walked most places and tried to avoid using the crowded Tube (underground). Finally, we had no choice but to use the Tube and we crowded onto an already busy train. As we neared our destination, I loudly communicated that the next stop would be ours. We arrived at our station and all piled off onto the platform as I hurriedly started a head count, hoping for 27 young players. No matter how many times I counted, I only came up with 26! One young man was still on the train!

In semi-panic, I left the parents in charge and ran to the nearest Tube official and explained what had happened. Calmly, he took me through a nondescript door into a room with a huge bank of mini TV screens showing a large number of their stations. Sitting on a chair facing this daunting barrage of technology was a pale faced insipid older gentleman smoking a cigarette. He was quickly told of my dilemma and "sprang into action." Laconically he targeted the route of the train we had just disembarked. He calmly called ahead and ordered the station which was its next port of call to search for my missing young man. Almost too easily, he achieved the seemingly impossible. I saw my missing player appear on one of his screens. My relief was palpable. Within minutes my group was whole again. I thanked my savior, and in true American fashion, gave him an enormous tip. No tip could compare to the cost of a law suit for losing somebody's son on the London Underground System.

Since arriving back from that eventful tour, I have met several of the boys and girls (now adults) who participated on that vacation. Their stories of what actually happened without my knowledge are too graphic to put into print. Impossibly, on the journey to England on the plane, there had been extensive sexual activity despite the presence of several parents acting as group supervisors. Although I have taken several England tours since, I am adamant that neither older teenagers nor older male and female groups will be given the opportunity to travel on my tours again.

Before returning to the USA I had effected a huge change in my father's life in Manchester by replacing his ancient phone with something out of the current century.

The old phone required you to stick your finger in the required hole and twist to the right, clockwise. Trying to call back to my wife in America was a nightmare requiring twelve twists of the wheel. Halfway through dialing, my finger would usually get stuck and I would have to start again. I replaced the phone while my father was out shopping for cigarettes. When he arrived back in his house, his eyes flickered toward the modern push-button phone sitting on the table in his hallway. Pretending not to notice, he lit up his cigarette.

"New phone, Dad," I offered brightly.

"Really," was his less than enthusiastic reply.

"Easier for you to use when you call me after I return to the States" (He had never called me in the 12 years I had been gone.)

"Bullocks! I only use the phone to call a taxi to take me to the British Legion." He's a great Dad I thought lovingly as the plane taxied ready to take me and my motley crew back to San Diego.

Youth Soccer – The Great Moments, Players , and Parents

It would be unfair and inaccurate to only describe the negative, cynical, political side of youth soccer in the USA. During my first twelve years involved in the youth soccer scene, there were many funny, exciting experiences provided by lovable kids and their supportive parents.

At one soccer camp, I had a group of 5 and 6 year old, sitting quietly in front of me and I was telling them the story of Noah and his Ark with the animals going on the ship two by two. One little boy kept putting up his hand during the story and I gently encouraged him to wait until the end. When the story ended, I invited him to ask his question.

"Coach, were you also on Noah's Ark?" the child asked eagerly.

"No," I replied with a smile on my face. The little boy looked confused, and then put up his hand again.

"If you were not on Noah's Ark, how come you didn't drown?" Out of the mouths of babes …..

A favorite activity during soccer camp lunch-break was the Joke of the Week contest. It always surprised me how willing the youngsters were to get up in front of their peers and tell jokes. It also surprised me the types of jokes they came up with. Here is a sample of some of the Joke of the Week soccer camp winners.

A small boy stood up in front of the class at school and said to the teacher,

"Please, Miss, I want to go for a poo."

The startled teacher replied, "It would be nice if you said you want to go for a No. 2."

A few minutes later another little boy stood up and said, "Please, Miss, I want to go to take a pee."

The teacher shook her head and calmly stated, "It would be nice if you said I want to go for a No. 3."

Toward the end of the lesson, Johnnie, the class clown, stood up and said, "Please, Miss."

"Yes, Johnnie. What do you want?"

Johnnie, smiling, replied, "It's not me Miss. It's Peter. He wants to fart but he doesn't know the code number!"

Not a bad joke for a nine year old to tell.

My own son, Ben, had me laughing out loud when he was 5 years old, playing in the Pacific Beach Recreation League. I asked him how he had played that morning.

"It was great, Dad! I scored 11 goals!" he shouted excitedly.

"Wow! That's fantastic! What was the final score?" I

asked.

"We won 8-0," he answered with the honesty and naiveté of a small child.

We also ran lunch competitions similar to the current show "America's Got Talent," resulting in kids bringing in their dogs, cats, and even a horse to entertain the other players at the soccer camp. My own favorite winnner was a little boy named Cole who used no props or jokes but thrilled his peers with a mime of using a needle and thread to manipulate his lips. The photos are hilarious!

Probably the most subtle joke to make the group laugh was told at one of my camps in Mammoth Lakes.

The teacher put her hand into a large shopping bag and said, "I can feel something round and I can see it's reddish. What is it? Alan?"

"It's a tomato," replied Alan.

"No. It's an orange, but your answer shows your thinking," complimented the teacher who then said, "I am holding something round, smooth, and green colored. What is it? James?"

"It's an apple, Miss," answered James hopefully.

"No, it's a melon, but it shows your thinking," said the teacher encouragingly.

Suddenly, little George stood up. "Can I have a go please, Miss?" he asked eagerly.

"Certainly," responded the surprised teacher.

"Well, Miss, I have my hand in my pocket and I am holding something two inches long and it's red at the end," said the boy enthusiastically.

The disgusted teacher pointed to the door. "Outside, you naughty boy!"

With a smile on his face, the boy replied, "Actually, Miss, it's a matchstick, but it shows your thinking!"

"It Never Rains but it Pours!!"

I had ill-advisedly purchased the real estate company where I had worked for ten years and quickly found that owning a business was not my strength. In addition, the real estate market collapsed immediately after I took possession (No, it did not collapse because of me!). I was losing thousands of dollars a month as sales plummeted, especially in the Mission Beach and Pacific Beach area which was our primary market.

Coaching at the Surf, working hard as head coach at the Lazers, trying to learn how to run the real estate company was taking me down a rocky path quickly. At the Surf, one of the mothers of my under eight boys team was constantly sniping and criticizing me for being "too hard" on her son who was truly a "star" player (my words, not hers). I also had a dilemma with the same team with my weakest player being the son of an extremely powerful business leader in the San Diego corporate world.

At the Lazers, my success in building the program had now alerted the Nomads to a potential Trojan horse in its midst. The huge monthly losses of my real estate company were keeping me awake at night wondering how to staunch the bleeding.

One redeeming feature was the warmth and support I was receiving from my friends from Rancho Santa Fe whose children played on my U/11 boys' team.

Over the months, my selfish behavior began to cause, understandably, serious problems at my family home. My wife was incredibly supportive of us working things out. Finally, inevitably, it was obvious that I had no right to be living at my family home under the circumstances I had created. With sadness and a heavy heart, I moved out of my family home, and fortunately, I was offered a guest house to live in in Rancho Santa Fe, on the grounds of one of my player's parents. It was a wonderful estate with five acres of fruit trees, a breathtaking 10,000 square foot home, tennis court, pool/spa and a superb detached guest house. It was far more than I deserved, but with the money disappearing fast down an "empty hole" at the real estate company, it was a welcome surprise.

My downhill slide continued quickly when I heard a whisper that there was a move to get me removed from my job as Lazers head coach. At the next meeting of the La Jolla Soccer League, I was voted out by a Board comprised mainly of people who didn't know me or anything about the Lazers or my contribution to the rapid progress of that organization. One of the lady members was, however, a mother of a child who had played unsuccessfully at the Lazers. The boy had moved on from our club, but the mother was a "Desperate Mom." It pays not to have enemies in high places.

I was truly mystified on what grounds the La Jolla Board had decided to fire me.

The day after losing my job at the Lazers, I received a strange phone call from a guy called Ron. He had been one of the Board members the previous evening who had voted to get rid of me. A "Desperate Dad?" No, the opposite. Ron had uneasy feelings about the previous night's decision and had phoned several friends of his who had children playing in the Lazers. Their input was in total disagreement to what Ron had heard at the Board meeting. Ron asked to meet me at the French Pastry Shop on La Jolla Boulevard and chat over a cup of coffee. I was impressed immediately by Ron and forever grateful that he took the time to apologize. To this day, we are still close friends.

Antigua/Paradise with the Society Elite

With everything falling apart almost daily, I was happy to accept an invitation from one of my Rancho Sante Fe parents. This lady, Audrey, was the "World's Greatest Organizer" who annually arranged for a large group of families to vacation together abroad. Past and future trips were to include Turks and Caico, Australia, and this particular year, Antigua. I had met Audrey through my Surf, Rancho Santa Fe group. I managed to help her son work his way back into a higher level of soccer and rebuilt his confidence in his athletic ability. The group consisted of many of the wealthiest families in La Jolla, Del Mar, and Rancho Santa Fe who in many cases knew each other. Many of their children went to private schools together such as Bishops, La Jolla Country Day, and Santa Fe Christian. Many also knew each other through their sports teams, especially soccer; hence my invite.

At the best of times, I was never in the same financial level as all the families who were to vacation together in Antigua. Even sending my sons to any of these private schools was way beyond my financial capability, even while I was living with my wife. At this time, struggling with my real estate financial crisis, I was definitely the "pauper" of the group. I had also made what was to be a set of crucial decisions, thanks to the advice of Audrey. She was, in addition to her group vacation planning talents, a very high respected family counseling psychologist. She had encouraged me strongly to spend time alone, living in the guest house, when I did not have my sons with me. Also, she had insisted that I give my social life a break while I "cleared my head (and conscience)." Finally, she strongly advised that I avoid alcohol during the painful divorce process and focus on my coaching and physical and mental fitness. Fortunately for the trip I had enough air miles to cover my round trip flight to Antigua and the all inclusive hotel/food/drinks deal.

The St. James Resort in Antigua was breathtakingly beautiful with its calm, protected harbor and the great expanse of blue ocean seemingly "around the corner." Within a day of arriving, I had recognized and met a couple of dozen families of children I had coached in years past. Most were delighted, if surprised, to see their former soccer coach in such esteemed environs. Not so pleasant were the few parents who did not have pleasant memories of my coaching. One mother insisted I "apologize to her son for ruining his soccer career" (where had I heard this before!). She was discomfited to see me, a lowly soccer coach, amongst her elite friends in this five star paradise in the Caribbean. I could almost read her mind, wondering where I had gotten the money to afford this trip. I was tempted to ask, "What soccer career I had I ruined?" Her son showed little interest in playing soccer and as the La Jolla Lazers teams improved, he was never able to compete. No point, clear mind, simple life, enjoy Antigua, avoid stress, and let my emotions clarify before returning to San Diego and the challenges that lay in wait.

Dinner was a formal meal of mouth-watering food served in a restaurant overlooking the glistening, smooth water of the Bay. As I was the only single guy in their large group, Audrey invited me to sit at her table. As I looked around the other people at the tables, I was in elevated company indeed! Opposite me was one of American's finest sports TV commentators, Dick Enberg and his lovely wife, and nearby was one of America's top hotel moguls, Doug Manchester and his delightful wife, Betsy. I had had the pleasure of coaching the Manchester's son, Douglas, Jr., and felt very comfortable that they were not on the

Desperate Soccer Parents list (thank goodness!). Also in the group was the owner of one of America's biggest Mercedes dealers, a highly respected family in the San Diego business community and a great gentleman.

I started to look at these wealthy, successful families around the elegant dining room and felt a strong sense of loneliness. With my divorce proceeding and without my sons on the trip, I was a somewhat pathetic figure. Interestingly, my reputation as a "dynamic soccer coach," seemed to provide the key for me to be accepted in the group as somewhat of an equal. For the first time since 25 years earlier when I had met Pauline, I was alone. I was surrounded by many families, but alone. I was in the midst of a breathtaking paradise, but lonely, with no one to blame but myself.

As the week passed by, I found that with not drinking alcohol and no girlfriend or wife at my side, I was actually beginning to feel a sense of peace that was unusual for me. Reading books, swimming in the Bay, sightseeing alone, and sometimes getting to know different families, my days ended with an unusual sense of calm.

On the last night in the casino, I was casually watching players gambling in the casino. I have never gambled, smoked, or "done drugs." In fact, my story was "It was drugs, alcohol and wild women that killed my grandfather. He couldn't get any, so he shot himself!!!"

From behind me I heard a woman's friendly voice ask me, "Are you winning or losing?"

"Neither. I don't gamble, but I find it interesting to watch people's behavior as they begin to lose their money," I replied.

"Same with me," this attractive, well dressed lady replied amicably. From the stunning jewelry to her stat- uesque posture, this was a woman of substance. Idly we chatted as the night progressed and a waiter appeared asking if we wanted to order any drinks.

"Champagne please," she ordered politely.

"Tonic water with ice and lime," I requested.

"Not drinking tonight? Hangover?" she inquired.

"No. A mind-cleansing exercise as I work my way through some challenging problems," I answered honestly. Gradually we learned more about each other and several hours passed quickly. She noted the Nike soccer shirt I was wearing, and I told her I was a professional soccer coach. She laughed and said she had children who had played.

The next day was time for my return to San Diego with two long flights waiting for me. I thanked her for her company, and she asked me if I would mind walking her back to her place. "It's so nice to talk to a gentleman who is sober and actually listens to what a lady is saying for a change," she complimented. I happily agreed to escort her back to her "room," and we departed the casino together. We walked casually along the romantically lighted pathways, listening to the boom of the nearby ocean as the waves crashed on the rocks. Heading away from my hotel to another part of the bay, we rounded a corner and I saw a beautiful, pink mansion perched on the cliff overlooking the expanse of the Bay. As she looked at this beautiful piece of architecture, she groaned, "Oh no, my kids are back already! Where are you staying?"

"I am staying at the hotel," I responded, still in awe of the grand palace in front of me.

"Great. Let's go back to the hotel together," she suggested. By now my eyes were fully opened and my mind was trying to take in this developing scenario.

"Are you married?" I asked. "No, divorced. I live in several of our homes around the world, depending on my children's school commitments."

I felt overawed and even threatened by the magnitude of her social and financial standing and my current financial and family crises. Fortunately my mind, alcohol free and clear, allowed me to look at this lady with, for me, unusual clarity. She was unpretentious and self-effacing, with no attempt to impress me with her wealth.

She had laughed when I had told her of my many experiences with Desperate Soccer Moms and Dads. She was herself a soccer mom. She explained that her ex-husband was a classic Desperate Soccer Dad who had regularly embarrassed her with his rantings up and down the sideline. "I have been so embarrassed to see the behavior of my husband and other of our friends on the sidelines of our children's soccer games. How can successful, intelligent adults lose their composure over a kid's soccer game? The ultimate was to see him red carded at my daughter's recreation game! He was dismissed by a thirteen year old boy who was refereeing the game. It was pathetic." We laughed together and arrived at the hotel.

She was calm, cool, and showed no reluctance as we entered my room. She had a magnificent, athletic body, honed by hours of Pilates, tennis and horse riding. Several hours later, in no hurry as she had staff living at her Bayside home overseeing her children, she started to take her leave. "Don't worry. I will get the hotel staff to drive me back to my place on one of the golf carts. I have had a wonderful evening. I would like to fly you back to San Diego in my jet plane tomorrow. I can have the pilots ready by early afternoon." Finally, I asked her for her name and what her ex-husband did for a living. I wished I had never asked! He was one of the richest entrepreneurs in Nevada and California who allegedly had links to people I would not want to upset. With my life already in turmoil, my sobriety surely saved me from accepting an offer which I should surely have refused. I said a reluctant goodbye, and the next day flew back to California on a "regular scheduled flight" to confront my demons.

Another bonus in Antigua occurred when I stopped to watch a family playing a pick-up soccer game on the beach. They were extremely friendly and invited me to join in their game. I enjoyed playing and when we stopped to get a drink, they said they were impressed by my soccer ability (a rare occurrence I admit). For the remainder of the vacation, I played in their soccer games which began to attract many other players. A friendship developed and they invited me to stay at their home with them in Upstate New York should I visit the East Coast.

Six months later, one of my San Diego soccer parents who was a senior pilot with American Airlines offered me a free round-trip flight to Newark. I contacted my new friends in New York who were delighted to hear from me and happy to house me during my visit. My soccer coaching network also gave me another added bonus with one of my parents, Brad DeLuiso being the kicker for the NFL New York Giants. I had coached Brad when he was at high school and was now coaching his stepson. Brad was kind enough to invite me and my host to watch the Giants play the Dallas Cowboys during my stay in the New York / New Jersey area. For a humble soccer coach, the chance for a free, thrilling vacation to the East Coast during the beautiful Fall season was a dream come true.

The only thing to undermine this great adventure was that Brad got seriously injured during the game trying to tackle Deion Sanders. Consequently, Brad and I didn't get an opportunity to meet after the game or during my stay. I am happy to see Brad still working out at my gym in Carmel Valley, San Diego. He still looks fit enough to play in the NFL.

"Know Thine Enemies" – Goodbye Surf

Shortly after arriving back from my trip to Antigua, I was coaching my young team at the Surf. We were actually playing up a year in age, and my weaker players were really struggling to cope. The mother of the weakest player mentioned on a couple of occasions that her son "would benefit from more playing time!" This was an upper class euphemism or diplomatic way of gently threatening a coach, especially when your husband is a highly influential senior member of one of San Diego's biggest businesses. I obviously didn't register the threat, which was to prove a fatal omission on my part.

Not surprisingly, my mate, Colin, had settled into the Surf well. His professional coaching improvement and growing maturity found him collecting supporters within the Club. He had found his niche, doing a fantastic job coaching girls teams and showing a real affinity to getting along well with the challenges of coaching young ladies. He had settled down and was now dating the mother of one of the girls who had played on a top Nomads boy's team! The girl went on to play for the National Women's team and in the Women's pro league. Colin's new partner was a fantastic "rock" for him to develop himself and his coaching career within the Surf Club.

Toward the end of the season, the local league "Presidio Cup" arrived, and I was excited for my young under eight boy's team to try and become the champion of the San Diego Cup, playing against boys a year older. In truth, in those days I was too emotionally committed to winning, and on many occasions, "lost the plot" (lost control of my emotions). This was still an ongoing problem for many pro youth soccer coaches and can be seen even in the recreation soccer games.

My little guys battled their way through group play and the semi-final against much bigger, stronger players. It was a pleasure to watch! Feisty, fearless, amazingly skilled – my little guys surprised their opponents, and we arrived in the Final with high hopes.

Before the Final, a mother, a single parent, voiced her displeasure at her son's limited playing time in the semi-final. I listened patiently as I heard the normal, predictable words that I have heard with thousands of variations over the many years. "How can my son get better if he is only on the field for a couple of minutes?" was the plaintiff inquiry from the mother.

The final was "men against boys" with our opponents far bigger and stronger, and their coach obviously (and intelligently) had told his team to "play physical." It made it a great game because my little guys played fearlessly, and half time rolled around with the game tied 0-0.

With the second half battle looming, I faced the inevitable decision. Do I keep my best players on the field, or do I use the weaker players off the bench? As I discretely glanced over at the listening parents, the single mother and the high powered father and his wife were looking at me with icy stares. Decision made! I would keep on the stronger, "starter" players who had done so well in the first half. I could almost feel the angry stares burning into my back.

The second half was a mirror of the first, with the skill and speed of my tiny warriors against the power of the older opponents. I could now see some of my players were tiring, so I called on the bench players to get ready. The son of "Mr. Influential" causally got off the bench and lethargically ambled toward me. I was not impressed, and distracted from the game, said somewhat cynically, "When you can move at a soccer speed, try again. Now sit back down!" A few seconds later, I felt a touch on my shoulder.

"I didn't appreciate what you just said to my son," said the well dressed, imposing father. In the Heat of Battle, I am not known for wit and repartee.

"Tough" was my ill-advised response. A couple of minutes later, I tried again with my substitution. This time the youngster moved quicker – relatively speaking. With the game hanging by a thread, 0-0, I sent my substitute on the field with one final instruction. "Hustle and work hard!" In less than two minutes, the player didn't move to the ball, lost possession, and his opponent ran through and scored. My next action sealed my fate. "Ref. Sub please!!!" I screamed. Pointing to my recent substitute, I said, "Thank you. Have a rest!" Many years later, I cringe as the whole scene plays back again in my mind. The young boy trundled off the field and slumped back onto the bench. The final whistle blew and we had lost 1-0.

A fantastic effort, marred by my indelicate coaching approach. The loss could have been a "Triumph of Effort," but my anger was only too apparent. I was inviting trouble, and I got it. As I turned, I faced the parents of my "failed" substitute.   In a calm, moderate voice, the father looked me in the eye and asked,

"Why was my son on the field for two minutes?" In a biting response, I childishly and unprofessionally fired back,

"Because I couldn't get him off any sooner." At the right moment, this old quip can get a few laughs. In this instance, I had denigrated an eight year old boy, and then exacerbating my unforgivable behavior, sarcastically tried to belittle two caring, quality parents who loved their son. To make matters worse, this same mother had regularly invited my own two sons back to their beautiful family home in Del Mar! The father looked at me with disdain, slowly shook his head, and with his arm gently around his wife's shoulder, they walked away from me. I had turned triumph into disaster. Defeat into Disgrace – mine!

Little did I know that I set in motion the end of my coaching career at the Surf soccer club.

The Ultimate Soccer Problem – Dangerous and Very Desperate

Because I was heavily involved on the competitive level of soccer, my only real interaction with young recreational players occurred during my summer soccer camps. When my own two sons were old enough to attend, it gave me great pleasure to watch them enjoying themselves.

I was waiting for the arrival of my friends from England who were coming to work with me at my summer soccer camps - three great athletes who were successful Physical Education teachers and great guys. I had enjoyed their message the previous day, explaining that they had missed their connection in Chicago and would arrive a day late. When they called my home, they heard the answering machine with my voice. In the 1980's, answering machines were unheard of in England, and my 3 mates were mystified what to do or how to handle the obvious.

"This is the house of Jeff and Pauline Illingworth. Please leave your message at the beep." Three bright guys with teaching degrees, but I heard Steve say,

"It's Jeff's voice, but he's not there." His voice was incredulous, as though something mystical was happening. It was a recording for Pete's sake! When they finally arrived, I gave them some grief.

During their first camp I introduced Vince, one of my English coaches, to the mother of one of his young players. The mother was very attractive and I could see there was a connection between them. I knew the husband and I was no admirer of the man. He had once told me that he and his wife had an "open marriage," and that he basically did whatever he wanted. Late that day Vince told me that the mother had invited him to meet in downtown San Diego for "happy hour." I had mixed feelings about it but Vince was single and the mother told him that she and her lowlife husband were splitting up.

Vince had a great evening and came home to my house with a smile on his face, in love with this stunning Californian beauty. I was happy for him but had an uneasy feeling particularly knowing what a nasty guy her husband was. All went well for a couple of days until the husband turned up at the soccer camp. Marching straight toward me, he pushed his face close to mine.

"How does your friend enjoy screwing my wife?" he hissed. "You British coaches think you're hot shots with your accents and fancy words," he continued. I tried to remain calm and not show my disgust for the man standing in front of me. Finally he stormed off the field. I walked across to Vince and told him what had happened. He was stunned but insisted that the mother had categorically stated that the marriage was over and she was at liberty to do what she pleased. I warned Vince to be careful and to tell the mother about the incident. At my house later he called the mother and seemed happy with the result, arranging to meet her later that evening at some secluded rendezvous.

Late that night I heard a knock on my bedroom door with Vince's voice sounding stressed. I joined him in the living room and he explained in a panic-stricken voice how the husband had appeared silently during the evening and was watching them through the wife's car window. Vince and the wife were both mystified about how the husband had found them.

I firmly advised Vince to end the relationship and move on to find another lady from the many beautiful girls in San Diego. Two days later we all departed for a camp in Mammoth Lakes and I thought we were in the clear.

Unfortunately the wife would not let the relationship end and continued to contact Vince. Foolishly, they arranged for her to come to Mammoth and they would rendezvous in a local hotel. They were confident that the husband would not be able to find them several hundred miles away from San Diego.

Without my knowledge, the tryst was set for the Tuesday evening and Vince disappeared on his own to meet the Desperate Soccer Mom. By sheer chance, the mom called home to San Diego and discovered that her husband had taken their kids for a "fun trip to Mammoth Lakes." Her cleaner had overheard the husband telling the children they were all going "to meet mom in Mammoth" The mother managed to get to Vince before he entered the hotel and they both waited and watched. Their meeting time had been 4:00 PM, and eerily at 4:20, the husband's car pulled up outside the hotel with the two children sitting in the back seat. The husband and the children got out of the car and entered the hotel office. Shortly after, they all reappeared with the husband carrying a room key. Vince and the mother stared with horror as her husband and children climbed the stairs and headed toward the room they had originally arranged to use. The husband, with a twisted smile on his face, quickly slipped the room key into the door and then threw the door wide open. To his utter dismay and obvious disappointment, the room was empty. He stormed downstairs to the office to try and find out what had happened.

Impossible as it seems, he wanted to catch his wife in an embarrassing situation and have his children there to share the moment.

When Vince arrived back at our motel and told me the story, I was appalled and frightened. I also questioned how the husband had discovered where his wife had gone, and even more troubling was how he knew their hotel. The wife had told Vince that her husband had been fired from the police and he had background experience as a detective. We were to eventually discover that he had his wife's phone "bugged" and was monitoring her calls. Thankfully Vince did not have a mobile phone so she had not called him to stop him from going to the hotel room.

Even with Vince's infatuation with this beautiful lady, this frightening incident was enough for him to realize he was "playing with fire." The mother headed back to San Diego by a circuitous route, careful to avoid her husband. Vince eventually calmed down and joined the rest of my coaching staff, enjoying our week in the glorious town high in the Sierra Mountains.

Many years later, I should mention, I occasionally see the mother and the father who are still together living their strange existence as though nothing had happened. It was a truly frightening experience, and I stay well away from the odd couple. Vince is now happily married with children of his own.

Two Final Triumps at The Surf Club

1. Dallas Cup 1994

My older Surf U/16 boy"s team had produced a magnificent season, and we were all thrilled to be headed off to The Dallas Cup. I had a talented group with my Captain Darren and leading defender a 16 year old "man" who led by example. Secretly we all felt that maybe we could bring back the first ever Dallas Cup Trophy for The Surf Club. Everybody was aware that on my last Dallas trip with the Nomads, I had come home a winner. Little did I realize that this would be my last tournament as a Surf coach?

The tournament began with us playing a skillful team from Mexico who was clearly superior in technique and soccer finesse. However, we were undoubtedly quicker, more athletic, and aggressive. We came away with a tie and a good learning experience against a different style of play than we were used to seeing in the USA. Our second game was against a solid American team, and we were worthy winners 2-0. Our final game was against a team from Brazil – one of the great soccer clubs in the world – Sao Paulo!

As I coach, I have often been criticized for not running intense, highly organized pre-game warm ups. Obviously, I have argued that my results over the many years prove my methods are effective and successful. As I looked across the field at our opponents, I was mesmerized by the incredible choreographed routine of the South American teenage soccer professionals. Only the Samba music was missing as this group of supremely athletic soccer players jogged, skipped, stretched, and jumped in unison. Even their soccer uniforms looked sharper and more impressive than any other uniform on the field around us. I felt strange as I watched and fell under the spell of this incredibly unique and intimidating warm up routine. Never before, or since, have I as a coach been overawed or influenced by the warm up of an opposing team.

Coming from California, a place full of tall, athletic people, I was stunned to compare my players with our Brazilian opponents. They were on average taller, fitter, and more athletic than us. They had beautiful, sun tanned skin with sparking white teeth and easy, relaxed smiles. Surely, I reasoned, they can only run so fast or jump so high as any other top 16 year old. No way could they physically manhandle us. I was now full of adrenaline, fuelled by excitement, and I must admit, a little fear.

The game started and I was transported into "another world" of soccer beyond anything I had ever seen in my many years of coaching youth soccer. I had always been a huge admirer of the many great Brazilian National teams and their gifted soccer heroes. Pele, Garrincha, Jairzinho, and Rivelino were players I had idolized in my youth and tried to emulate – unsuccessfully. Here in front of me, I was privileged to watch these magnificent Brazilian youngsters, many of whom would surely go on to be top class professional players. It was amazing to watch my own players, who I had seen win so many games in California, made to look so ponderous and "wooden." Despite their enormous efforts, my players were totally outclassed. We managed to score a goal from a great free kick, but finished up losing 6-1.

The Sao Paulo team advanced to the Final without giving up any other goals in all their other games. We had something to be proud of! We had scored a goal against them!

I watched the Dallas Cup Final with great anticipation on TV back home in San Diego. The totally different styles of Sao Paulo and their Italian opponents from Super Club

Inter- Milan were fascinating to watch. The Italian team was highly organized in defense, conservative in attack, and seemed to be wary of getting overrun by the Brazilians. Certainly the fact that teams were made up full time professionals was a great leveler, and the game was a tough struggle for the Brazilians. Nevertheless, the inevitable happened. After a surprise goal by Inter-Milan, the Brazilians scored, then quickly added another to win 2-1. Worthy champions!

The whole Dallas Cup experience that year had been a great soccer education for me, showing just how good players have to be to play at the highest professional level.

2. Surf Cup Gala Night
Parents, Leave Your Desperation Behind for a Night

All competitive soccer clubs, especially those with paid professional clubs, are in reality businesses with a budget to be balanced. The main source of revenue is obviously the annual fees paid by the families of the players. In Southern California, many of the top clubs charge between $1,500 and $2,500 per player. This often does not include tournament fees, hotels, club/team camps, and post season training. Competitive youth soccer is a huge financial, time, and emotional strain on the families involved. For the elite teams, additional costs can include Regional and National tournaments all over the USA.

During my many years in teaching and coaching, I had been instrumental in organizing successful fundraising Gala Nights to raise money for my club teams or school. I suggested to the President of The Surf Club that we arrange a Gala Night to add something extra to the soccer side of our organization. He seemed a little anxious or intimidated at taking on such a huge venture and began to demur. Quickly I assured him that I would oversee the whole event, including location, entertainment, and food. We agreed that I would receive a "token" monetary reward of 10% of the net profit for my efforts.

While discussing the Gala Night with my friends from Rancho Santa Fe whose boys played for me, I "won the lottery." The lady who had kindly allowed me to live in their beautiful guest house offered her stunning home to host the event. Challenge number one overcome! The entertainment was also quickly arranged. My favorite non-desperate dad, Bob, in addition to being a very successful stockbroker, was also a talented musician. He played keyboards in an excellent band that performed regularly at clubs, weddings, and fundraisers all around San Diego. He offered the band to us for free. Now for the food. I was temporarily leading a charmed life! When news of the Gala reached the families in the club, I received a call from a parent "angel" (yes, not all soccer parents are desperate!). This gentleman owned a top seafood restaurant in nearby Del Mar. He was offering to supply all the food, catering, and serving staff for our event – FOR FREE!

Now came time for the fine details of organizing this huge event, especially parking for 450 people. The host family's home was a 10,000 square foot Estate on 5 acres situated on a quiet street near the Village. Parking was not allowed on their street. The windows opened completely like a Hawaiian Hotel to emphasize the superb view over the tennis court and rows of lime and lemon trees.

The event must have been destined to succeed because a second "angel" appeared in the form of Audrey. She was the lady who had organized the multi-family trip to Antigua. A superb organizer, highly intelligent, forceful, and dynamic, she assumed the mantle of Leader. With my 15 years experience in show business in England, I was happy to m.c. the Event, including the live and silent auctions. With the band providing the musical entertainment, I would provide the comedy and humor – I hoped.

Over the several months of organizing, we met regularly at Audrey's elegant home and sat in awe as she meticulously planned The Event. By now it was apparent that The Gala was going to be a huge success and raise a large amount of money for The Surf Club. To be honest, when I worked out the financial details of the fundraiser, I realized that the net profit on the evening may be more than $75,000. I confess that my 10% potential reward was a windfall I had never envisioned when I first mooted the idea of a fundraiser.

During a drink break at a meeting at Audrey's home, the Club President (unfortunately no longer Mike Connerley) followed me into the kitchen. "This Gala is going to make some serious money from the way things look right now," he said. Taking this as a compliment, I smiled, gave the two thumbs up sign, and replied positively,

"Absolutely - beyond my wildest dream! You better start working out what you and your Board are going to do with all the money." A dark shadow passed across his face as he looked at me in a surprisingly hostile way.

"You stand to make a fortune out of this for doing almost nothing," he accused. He was not only a Desperate Dad, but one who was the President of The Club and my boss! I was truly stunned by his words, and the mood in the kitchen was threatening. Before I could respond, he blurted out,

"Your compensation will be capped at $5,000 irrespective of how much the net profit is from The Gala. That's more than enough for your efforts. Audrey has done all the work – not you!"

By now I had recovered my composure and was

seething at these biting insults. Bearing in mind my adversary Board position, I should have responded diplomatically and with a calm, reasoned argument. But oh no – not me! I proceeded to take another strike and further tighten the noose around my neck.

"You lying bastard! How dare you! The Club stands to clear more than $65,000 in profit after I am paid my share. That's $65,000 more than it would have in its account if I had not come up with the idea. The house was donated because of my close relationship with the host family. The band has offered its services for free because of my friendship with …."

"You're capped at $5000! Take it or leave it!" he shouted angrily, now totally out of control.

At that moment, Audrey dashed into the kitchen wondering what the shouting was all about. "What's the problem?" she asked calmly in a tone befitting what she was – a successful psychologist, specializing in family problems. For sure, we had a "family Surf problem."

"Simple, Audrey," I responded heatedly. "Our President wants to renege on an agreement we have had since day one. He wants to limit my share of The Gala profit from our agreed upon 10% to a maximum of $5000. I am disgusted by …."

"Give me five minutes, Jeff, if you please," she cajoled. I left the kitchen and returned to the living room where the other members of the organizing committee were sitting, surprised and uneasy. A few minutes later, both Audrey and the Club President entered the room and an uncomfortable silence pervaded the atmosphere.

"Let's continue, shall we?" Audrey ordered in her famous no nonsense manner. The President and I sat stiffly, darting eyes occasionally meeting each other's. It seemed absurd that we were all sitting there, organizing a

Huge Event for a non-profit soccer club with electricity in the air. Finally the meeting ended and the uncomfortable committee members hurriedly dispersed.

When there was only myself and Audrey left, she looked directly at me and said pointedly,

"You think you are 100% in the right, don't you? You were until you lost your control and used profanity to emphasize your displeasure. You have put yourself in an unenviable position. You will get your 10% as agreed. You have every right to it. However, you have gained a dangerous enemy who is in a position to do you real harm. With all that you have going on now with your divorce, the last thing you need is more drama in your life."

A chill ran through my body - a sense of foreboding, remembering my altercation with the powerful father after the Presidio Final a few months earlier. Two powerful, influential soccer dads desperately displeased with me did not augur well for my coaching career at The Surf Club.

Gala Night – Soccer Parents at Their Best

After several more planning meetings with Audrey, it was finally the night of the first Surf Gala. I arrived early, as requested, which was not difficult as I was living in the guest house only a few steps away. It was a beautiful Southern California evening with blue skies, gentle breezes, and the sun slowly setting over the nearby Pacific Ocean. Bob and his band had already set up their equipment and were ready to start playing to welcome the early guests. The evening would provide a unique opportunity for soccer parents from all the teams in the Club to get together. Away from the stress of games, 450 parents could mingle together with the coaches and the Board members. The host family had prepared their sumptuous home elegantly, opening the huge windows and doors facing west over the enormous garden and orchard. It was the ideal setting for such a large occasion, and with all the organizational details in hand, "Audrey style," we waited for the guests/parents to start arriving.

My job was full time MC carrying a portable microphone, promoting, and talking up the many inviting auction items. Several of the wealthier parents had donated their vacation homes in such beautiful locations as Hawaii, Sun Valley, Idaho, and Mammoth Lakes. Well known pro indoor soccer star, Julie Veee, had donated some of his superb paintings. I was stunned at the number of auction items which were laid out invitingly on long tables with embroidered cover sheets.

Finally the first guest arrived - the Club President and his wife!!! Unable to run and hide, I put on my best smile and greeted them warmly while shaking hands. The meeting was a little cool but not as unpleasant as I had feared. Quickly the room and pool area started to fill up as mini-buses shuttled groups of parents to The Gala. The mood was festive and there was a superb atmosphere developing as parents started to mingle freely. The father who had generously donated all the food and liquor had also provided a quality staff of servers.

My favorite Surf parent then arrived with his lovely wife. Mike Connerley and Sue climbed the elegant staircase with smiles on their faces. How I wished Mike was still President on this glorious evening. I had enjoyed coaching his son, Josh, and benefitted from Mike's sage advice over the past two years. He had been a great part-president and was now committed to his "invention" – The Surf Cup.

When all the guests/parents arrived, I invited everyone to get together in the enormous living room. With the microphone in my hand, I turned back the years to my time in England as a professional comedian.

"The USA Men's National Soccer Team was on a tour of Africa, playing friendly games. At the end of the tour, they played an all-star team of animals, including their captain – a lion, goalkeeper giraffe, and two speedy leopards playing out wide. At half time, the game was tied 0 – 0. When the second half began, the animal team had brought a centipede on as a substitute forward. Within five minutes, the centipede showed incredible dribbling skills and scored two quick goals. By the end of the game, the animal all-star team won 4 – 2 with all their goals being scored by the centipede. As they were all walking off the field, the two captains shook hands. The USA captain said to the lion, "Your substitution was a master stroke. The centipede was incredible! I must ask you, why didn't you play him during the first half?" The lion replied, "We wanted to but he was still busy tying up his laces!""

The parents enjoyed the joke and I warmed to the occasion, continuing with;

"It was kick off time in the Final of the English FA Cup in London with 100,000 soccer fans packed into the Stadium. Sitting in a prime seat on the half way line, a guy looks at the empty seat next to him. Surprised to see such a valuable seat empty, he spoke to the man on the other side of the vacant seat.

"It is amazing to me to see one of the best seats in the Stadium empty. I wonder who has the ticket for it." The other guy replied, "I do."

"Really? Why is nobody sitting in it?" asked the curious fan.

"The seat belongs to my wife but she died," said the second guy sadly.

"My sincere condolences. That is heartbreaking. However, I'm surprised you didn't offer your deceased wife's seat to one of your friends," asked the now intrigued first guy.

"I did offer the seat to several of my friends but they are all at my wife's funeral!"" The response to the joke was tremendous and I segued into the live auction.

"The first prize is a week's vacation in Pittsburgh. The second prize is a month's vacation in Pittsburgh!!!" Lots of laughter.

By the mood of the crowd, our hopes for a lively auction were high and we were not disappointed. Several items went for thousands of dollars. As we concluded the live auction, Audrey was beaming with a wide smile.

The problems with the desperate parent and desperate Club President seemed a million miles away.

Bob and his band struck up with some great music, and the dance area next to the swimming pool was quickly filled.

Audrey was everywhere, supervising the collection of

money from the auction items.

The hours raced by, and gradually the boisterous, happy soccer parents disappeared. The band finished, and before we finally left, I went to thank them for a job well done. My last act was to hug both Audrey for a job done superbly, and sincere gratitude to my "Good Samaritan Landlords" who had donated their home for this stunning Gala.

I took the short walk to the guest house with a spring in my stride and a contented smile on my face. It had been an evening successful beyond my wildest dreams, and I couldn't help thinking how much good it must have done for me within The Surf Club.

On the following Monday, as I arrived for training, I was delighted when the Club President walked up to me with a smile on his face. "You were worth every penny of the 10% we agreed on. The Gala was spectacular, and you and Audrey did a first class job." I felt ecstatic and relieved to hear those heartwarming words from some-body I had made into my enemy.

Fifteen years later, this gentleman is still a friend and still involved as a high level administrator of youth soccer. He has given freely thousands of hours of his time to sup-port youth soccer and is somebody I have grown to admire more and more as the years go by.

Sliding Toward the Abyss – Quickly

Eventually it was time for me to vacate the guest house of my generous benefactors since they had family coming to stay with them. Seriously short of money, as I was now paying child support for my two sons, I looked for a cheap place to stay. One of my coaching colleagues suggested that I might ask his girlfriend if I could rent a bedroom in her home. She had two sons about the same age as my boys and it may work well. I asked and she agreed willingly, so our arrangement was I would pay her $400 a month. With my child support payments, rent, and car payment, I was now over my income from the Surf coaching job.

My bedroom was a converted garage with a tiny bathroom and shower, no closets, and the mattress took up every inch of the tiny room. My clothes were laid in piles on the far edge of the bed. I took in this pathetic sight and the full impact of how dire my situation was fully hit me. Only a couple of years ago, I was living with my wife and two lovely sons in an elegant home near the Ocean, waking up next to a good wife and having breakfast with her and our children. My selfishness and stupidity had been responsible for my own demise. One night as I lay on the small bed with my two sons next to me sleeping, I cried pitifully. Ashamed of where I was, barely able to support my boys and even less able to truly support myself. If I were to lose the soccer coaching job, I really didn't see any way I could make any money other than minimum wage in a bar or fast food restaurant.

One life saving piece of good fortune occurred when I was able to offload the real estate office before I truly sunk. On chance, I phoned the owner of a nearby office of the same franchise. To my intense relief, he finally agreed to take over ownership which prevented any future fatal financial "bleeding."

I was still enjoying my teams, and the bright spot in my day was when I headed off to training each afternoon. There was, however, a feeling of pending disaster that I felt hanging over me. It was a feeling that was to come true, but in a manner I would never have wanted in my worst fears.

The Crash Landing!

Before my downhill slide, I had bought a pretty, white Infiniti 935 sedan which was a new, futuristic shape. I enjoyed taking my landlady's two sons to practice as they played at the same soccer club where I worked. On my days with my own two sons, it was fun to drive all four boys to practice. Leaving the home where I was renting, I headed along Governor Drive in University City toward the 805 Freeway.

With the boys laughing and joking loudly, we headed east on the wide, spacious road with minimal traffic. I noticed a large car starting to move slowly forward from a street on my right, about 70 yards in front of me. I touched my brakes and became cautious as I neared the now stationary car poking out a little from the now nearing street. Inexplicably, as I closed to within yards of passing her, the driver pulled out directly in front of me, trying to turn left.

Slamming on my brakes, I pulled hard to the left trying to avoid hitting the other car full on its driver's side. In a sickening blur of activity, my car sped inexorably toward the large Cadillac. The screams of the four boys ringing in my ears pierced through my sense of disbelief as we struck the other car at high speed – a sickening blow. The seat belts worked, and the two front safety air bags deployed, creating a surreal scenario inside my car. There was a strong "hospital smell" which was caused by the air bags.

When the cars came to a final stop, I began to quickly climb out of the car to survey the total damage to all the boys, both cars, and the other driver. Under duress, I had forgotten to put my car in park and apply the handbrake. My vehicle started to gather speed and roll forward. Fortunately, I managed to scamper back through the driver's door and secure the car.

The four boys were crying and screaming, and my son in the front seat was holding his face. The substance used to deploy the airbags had burned my son's face, and he was in acute pain exacerbated by his fear and state of shock. My other son and the landlady's two boys were frozen with fear as I tried to get all four out of the car. Fortunately, we had not been hit by any other cars as we had swerved across the oncoming lanes. I ran over to the other car, which was badly damaged and looked directly through the driver's side window. The elderly lady driver sat deathly still; eyes frozen, staring eerily, unblinking. I was sure she was dead. Maybe the force of the impact or the shock had led to a heart attack. From a distance, I heard the urgent, blaring sound of fast approaching emergency vehicles. The paramedics took over in a calm, professional manner as I stood in a daze watching the four boys dressed in their soccer equipment being treated. It was with a profound sense of relief that I saw the elderly lady from the other car being carefully extricated and carried to an ambulance. She was now distressed and crying violently with fear and realization as she looked plaintively at her destroyed vehicle.

I had by now recovered enough to call my ex-wife to tell her what had happened and which hospital we were being taken to. I had also called a coaching colleague to explain my absence. Later, my ex-wife came to take our sons back to her home, and I lay in my hospital alone. My body ached everywhere, especially my neck and back, and I started to shiver either with pain, fear, loneliness, or all three.

The next day I was released and gingerly climbed into the ambulance to be taken to my lodgings. With no car, I was isolated, unable to even get to the soccer fields to do my coaching.

My savior, "Gala Organizer Extraordinaire," Audrey called me to check on my health and kindly offered to loan me one of their "spare vehicles." To this day, I do not know how I would have managed without the incredible generosity of Audrey and her husband. I reflected deeply on my first meeting with her. She and her husband had been a classic Desperate Soccer Mom and Dad. Their son, a fine, all around athlete, had been "cut" from his local competitive soccer team despite the fact that his own father was involved as an assistant coach. Both Audrey and her husband were devastated to see their son parted from a team that included many of his close friends from their local community of Rancho Santa Fe.

On the recommendation of several of her friends who were parents of boys on my own team, I had made a huge effort over several months to help Audrey's son. He was a fine young man who I enjoyed coaching, and I felt a great sense of enjoyment when he eventually joined my team which included several of his good mates.

Never in my wildest dreams did I realize that these two Desperate Soccer Parents would become such vital sources of support and inspiration when I eventually reached my ultimate low point.

As One Door Closes, Another Slams Shut!

I found myself with my Infiniti a "total wreck," my neck and back sore and bruised, and headed to my Saturday games driving my "loaner" car – a Honda Accord. One of my younger teams was playing a vital game which would decide their league championship. I was "up" for the game and gave an impassioned pre-game motivational speech. "We have come so far, worked so hard in training, played so many tough games. This one game is for the championship which I truly believe you deserve…" Before I could finish my sentence, I was rudely interrupted by a female, loud, stentorian voice – "Cards!!!" she ordered.

I looked around for the source of this uninvited interruption. Standing immediately behind me with a stony face was an attractive, sun tanned lady dressed in a referee uniform. Her physical appearance belied her unfriendly, unyielding manner.

"Cards what?" I asked her in a chilled tone.

"I need your cards now to check in your players," she replied in a similar tone.

"Have you ever heard of the words, Please or Excuse Me?" I countered. We stared at each other with mutual, open disdain.

"I'm not here to argue with you!" she said dismissively. I looked at her face and there was something vaguely familiar in both her physical appearance and her behavior and attitude. Where had I seen her before?

"I was in the middle of my pre-game when you so rudely…"

"I want your cards now," she interrupted contemptuously. It hit me like an electric shock! She was "A Very Desperate Mom from the past! This lady had been the mom of a player who had played against one of our teams a year ago. At that game, she had complained loudly and bitterly about the referee (go figure!) and the rough play of our players. At that game she had been a nuisance; now she was the assistant referee of the game about to be played. It was obviously a dangerous, volatile mixture of circumstances. She obviously recognized me and made no effort to conceal her disdain.

I signaled casually to my team manager to come over and give the players' cards to this hostile official. Inevitably, when the game began, she was the assistant referee working my sideline. The importance of the game created a tense atmosphere, and both sets of parents were loud and involved. To make matters more inflammatory, the center referee was a teenager approximately 14 years of age. The poor kid was way out of his comfort level, and as the game lurched forward, both the opposing coach and I loudly questioned several of his decisions. Defending him aggressively, the Desperate Mom/assistant referee, warned me on several occasions to "Keep your mouth shut and your opinions to yourself." Hardly soothing advice designed to calm the situation.

It only needed a major incident to ignite this "powder keg," and in the second half, it occurred. We were losing 1 – 0 and desperately needed a goal to tie and get the point to win the League. Our opponents needed to win to get the three points they needed to win the League for themselves.

My forward darted into their penalty area with the ball, faking out one of their defenders completely. The defender left a foot out and my player tripped and fell badly. An obvious penalty! Both sidelines went crazy. "Foul! Penalty! Red Card!" screamed my parents. Normally I do not allow any parental interference but with "the assistant referee from hell" on our sideline, I needed all the support I could get. The other sideline tried everything to dissuade the young official from blowing for a penalty kick. "No Way! Accident! He dived! Fake!" The poor boy was terrified. I was furious and waited to see his decision. No whistle!

I admit I was out of order. I continued to voice my disgust vehemently. The assistant referee suddenly ran on to the field when the ball was out of bounds and spoke animatedly to the young referee. She was blatantly trying to coerce him into giving me a Red Card and dismiss me from the game. Fortunately for me, he pulled out a Yellow Card and gave me a warning, much to the disgust of his friendly assistant.

The game ended with our sideline frustrated, angry, and my parents desperately determined that I "Do Something" about the referee! I gathered my players together to console them in their moment of loss, and before I could say more than a few words, unbelievably, my nemesis chimed in –

"Your behavior was disgraceful. What kind of example did you set for your players? You failed …. " I was now beyond any point of reason.

"GET LOST!" I hissed, staring at her with unconcealed loathing.

Finally the players and parents departed and I looked over to see the young referee sitting on a bag crying with my enemy talking "at him." Now calm, I felt sympathy for the young official and genuine remorse for my behavior, despite the huge provocation of the Desperate Mom/assistant referee. I walked over to the distraught figure, and ignoring the "talking head," I put my hand on his shoulder.

"Listen, son. I am sorry for the manner in which I treated you during the game. It was an important game for both teams, and you were put in a very difficult, no win situation. Please accept my apologies." He looked up with tears running down his cheeks and whispered, "Thanks." As I walked way, I heard "the voice" yet again.

"Red Card him now before it's too late! Now! Before he leaves the field and is gone!" she implored. I dared not look back lest I saw or do something appalling that I would surely regret.

Leaving the field, a group of parents from the opposing team were talking animatedly amongst themselves. "Tough luck out there coach," one parent said genuinely. "That lady assistant referee is a jerk. We have her every week, and she treats everybody as if they were her servants," offered one mother. I chatted amiably with the opposing parents and we all bemoaned the poor situation. I drove home frustrated, but talking to such a great group of parents had taken some of the "sting" out of the situation. Or so I thought!

That night I got a call from a member of the Presidio Board which governs competitive youth soccer in San Diego County. He was an old friend, a non-desperate soccer dad, who willingly gave up his time to serve on various youth soccer boards.

"Jeff, I have some bad news for you. Apparently you were given a Red Card today after the game. What the heck was that all about?" I started to explain the situation, and as soon as I mentioned the name of the female assistant ref ...

"Oh no," he interrupted. "Dragon Lady. We hear her name on a regular basis. The problem, however, is the referee, who is only a teenager. It is an emotional situation, especially with all the referee abuse problems we deal with on a weekly basis. To make matters worse, the current

Presidio President is a believer in "capital punishment!" He is always looking to give out the toughest punishment allowed. When you come in front of the Board, show and express repentance and remorse. Do not even try to argue the correctness of your behavior or else you will be "hung, drawn, and quartered!"

I had two weeks to wait for my trial and the possible fate of my coaching career which would be in the hands of a group of soccer parent/volunteers. Overseeing them was the most feared Desperate Soccer Dad – one who was in charge of an influential decision making committee. I knew this particular man, and I was in no doubt that my future in coaching was in serious jeopardy.

The two weeks would pass slowly and uncomfortably as the news of my Red Card started to spread around the Club. When things couldn't get any worse, THEY DID! I was informed that I had to meet with the Board of my own Club a few days after my hearing with the Presidio trial board.

Youth Soccer Can Be Fun!

So many parts of my book so far have focused on the negatives that occur within the world of competitive youth soccer in the United States. I would be remiss if I did not extol the many virtues, joys, and humorous sides of our great game - again.

Coaching youth soccer for a living in San Diego is a job almost every soccer coach in the world would die for. Beautiful weather year round, motivated, talented youngsters, including some of the most gifted girls in the world.

At one of my soccer camps in La Jolla, a group of ten year old girls attended and proved to be a "once in a lifetime" ensemble. They were incredibly talented, had fabulous team dynamics, a great sense of humor, and all with a genuine passion for the game. The second week of my camp, the same group appeared again; full of energy and passion, playing hard every second of the camp. This talented group of young ladies who played for the Surf were to become the greatest girls team in Surf history. In the years that followed, they totally dominated their age group in San Diego, California, and the USA. To test themselves against stronger competition, they played in top boy's tournaments and won! They played girls one year older and won! They played girls two years older and won! I feel proud to have been involved in some small way to have been there at the beginning of their dynasty. The core of the team stayed together until they all went their own way on Scholarships to top colleges all over the USA. Talented? For sure. Determined and aggressive? Absolutely. But most of all, they were soccer loving, fun loving, caring young ladies – a team for all ages! If any of these ladies read this book, I give them my thanks for the joy they gave me.

Great credit must be given to my mate, Colin, who coached this team to greatness winning 16/17 Surf Cups, dozens of tournaments, and numerous League titles. His superb coaching and management of this team really showed how far he had come in his coaching career. The ultimate reward for Colin was becoming Head Coach of the Surf soccer club – a club he has taken to National and World prominence. I have great pride in having been a small part of Colin's great success.

Great U.S. Youth Players
Nicki Serlenga

While on the subject of great female players, I cannot ignore the opportunity to mention the greatest I ever saw and had the honor to coach on occasion. Nicki Serlenga was the only girl playing in a Nomads boys soccer team. Even in this elevated soccer level, she was a star despite her small, slight stature. In her early teens, she was composed, confident, and utterly without fear regardless of whom she was playing against. She had superb skills, lightning speed, and incredible balance – able to change direction instantly. Few players can be predicted to go on and play at professional level, or even international level. I had no doubt that Nicki would make the grade. While I was directing a camp in Mammoth Lakes, she joined me in a pickup game involving a group of men. By the end of the game, Nicki had acquired a new group of admirers. Quite simply, they were mesmerized by her talent, athleticism, and strength of character. No "shrinking violet" – she possessed a great sense of humor; could give and take a joke and did not know the word intimidation. Over the years I was honored to watch her go on to a hugely successful college career, success in the women's professional league, and several times on TV with the Women's National Team.

Jovan Kirovski

On the boy's side, I was delighted to hear that Jovan Kirovski had been scouted by the top team in the world – Manchester United. In fact, he gave up high school and courageously relocated to live in my former city, Manchester. I followed his progress at Manchester United, and on one of my trips home to Manchester, I went down to Salford to watch Jovan train.

Brian Kidd was the head United coach, and I walked over the field to say hello to him. Looking up at me without recognition, he informed me that I should not be on the field. We had known each other years earlier and grew up only a couple of miles apart.

"Kiddo, it's me, Goffer, from the Old Days!" Recognition dawned.

"Long time no see. What's going on with you?" he asked sincerely.

"I've been living in San Diego for many years coaching soccer. In fact, you have one of my former players over there training with the team. Jovan," I said proudly. A little surprised, he smiled and said,

"Let me introduce you to his coach, "Pop" Robson," "Kiddo" offered kindly. I spoke with "Pop" for a few minutes, and he spoke highly of Jovan, pointing out some areas of weakness but many positives.

Jovan was surprised to see me on that cold, windy Manchester day. I'm sure my presence brought back memories of warm, sunny days playing in La Jolla, overlooking the sparkling blue Pacific Ocean.

The following Saturday I had the opportunity to watch him play for United's youth team against local rivals, Manchester City. United won easily, playing in icy conditions and Jovan looked sharp, confident, and very much "at home." Sixteen years of age, living on a different continent, surrounded on a daily basis by some of the world's greatest and most famous soccer stars, Jovan was a quiet, modest young man who would never make enemies or cause any problems.

He worked his way steadily "up the ladder" at Manchester United, which is no easy task with all the elite competition. Eventually he played in the United Reserves Team and was a prolific goal scorer. It looked only a matter of time before he made his debut in the First Team. Unfortunately, United was unable to obtain a work permit for him. His father, Zivko, a close friend of mine, was Yugoslavian, and in those years, his native country was not a member of the European Economic Community (EEC). Consequently, Jovan and his family did not qualify for a work visa.

Jovan moved to a top European Club and finally, with enough international appearances for the USA Men's Team, he "qualified" to play in the English Premier League. He was bought by Steve Bruce, the former Manchester United captain who was manager of the EPL team Birmingham. In recent years, Jovan has returned to a successful career playing in the top American pro league – the MLS.

A sad note was the untimely death of his father, Zivko. Jovan's father was one of the nicest, most sincere soccer dads I have ever met. Despite the genius and talent of his son, Jovan, Zivko supported the "team concept" and never looked for or expected any special treatment for his son. The night Zivko brought Jovan to try out for my team at the Nomads, his humble words personified the quality of the man. "Coach, I would be honored if you would spare the time to give my son, Jovan, a tryout with your team."

On a lighter note, our mutual European backgrounds gave us a shared sense of humor. Our favorite joke was, "Whether you are Yugoslavian, French, German, British, or Italian, when you go to the toilet, Eur-o-pean."

Of the many great youth players I have had the honor to coach, none has been more humble or a greater team player than Jovan. His great, enduring pro soccer career is a testament to his hard work, dedication and talent.

Frankie Hejduk

During my time at the Nomads, I had the pleasure of watching a typical California Surfer Dude play with all his heart every practice and every game. Despite a tall, powerfully built father, Frankie was small in stature but possessing a giant personality. Lightning quick, boundless energy, and a driving passion for the game, he was impossible to miss when he was on the field. Often he would arrive with his hair wet from his other love – surfing! Whatever Frankie did, he gave 100%.

His pro career has been magnificent with several years playing in a top German league team, many appearances for the USA Men's National Team, and the honor of several World Cup appearances. Recently he returned to the USA and is performing superbly in the MLS. Only a few weeks ago I watched him lead the Columbus Crew to winning the MLS Cup. It was with great joy and pride that I watched him as the captain of that team hold, the trophy above his head.

Only a few weeks earlier, I ran into him in my local bar and restaurant in Del Mar, The Poseidon. He was the same old/young Frankie – energetic, dynamic, with long, flowing hair and a big smile.

TK Inbody and Chugger Adair – My Franchise Players

It is many years (28) since my arrival in San Diego and beginning my US coaching career at Mission Bay Soccer Club. Many of the memories make it seem like it was only a few days ago – maybe that's what happens as you approach 60 years of age. The importance of my first years in San Diego and my good fortune and luck in being hired at Mission Bay Soccer Club by Hank, remain with me.

I could never have built the Mission Bay Soccer Club without my "blind" good fortune of acquiring two superb young players with great supportive parents.

Chugger and his parents personified all that is opposite of Desperate Soccer Moms (and Dads). They were loving, caring, and supportive of their son; loyal and committed to me as the coach. My ex-wife, Pauline, and I spent many happy Christmas Eves and Christmas Days in the warm, welcoming Adair family home. I was there when Chugger graduated from sixth grade, sitting with his parents outside under a hot summer son. We all shared the heartbreak of our loss with the U/16 Hotspurs team in Albuquerque, New Mexico in the US Regional Final.

I followed Chugger's college career. He was the co-captain of USD when they defied all the odds and critics and reached the NCAA Final - a massive achievement for a college not regarded as big time!

After graduating, Chugger played for The Sockers Indoor Pro team and spent some time playing professionally in Europe.

He is now a happily married man with a family of his own and a successful college coach in his own right. Just to prove that "nice guys" do finish up winners!

TK graduated from Stanford and is now a very successful Hedge-Fund Executive in Northern California. During his college days, he once worked for me at one of my soccer camps. The kids at the camp loved him, and he would certainly have made a great soccer coach at any level – if he was willing to take a huge salary cut.

Trial by Jury

In my comedian days, there were many jokes about trials and juries. In Manchester in the 1960's, a famous gay comedian, Al S., upset the judge with his effeminate actions. The judge was not amused and threatened Al,

"Your homosexual display is about to get you in trouble." Famous for his quick, biting wit, Al replied,

"With all due respect, Your Honor, you are the only man in court wearing a wig!"

As I faced the soccer committee trial board, I felt no sense of peace or hope. The atmosphere was subdued, hostile in some quarters, and charged with a sense of drama. In front of me was a group of soccer dads and a mom who freely volunteered their time. Each of them did so for a variety of different reasons - some good, some not so good. I had one "friend" on the board – I hoped!

"Referee abuse is unacceptable and will not be tolerated by this board, PERIOD!!" thundered the President. Even the other board members were stunned by this vitriolic, verbal assault. Remembering the advice of the friendly board member weeks before, I kept my mouth closed – for a change!

"You are charged with continued abuse of a young referee in your U/10 game against N.C. soccer team two weeks ago. Despite persistent warnings from the assistant referee who continually tried to help you behave yourself," he accused. Thinking back to the rude, obnoxious lady assistant referee, I found it hard not to interject at this point. Looking at the President and the other board members in a dispassionate manner, I felt unbelievably alone. Over 15 years of being involved in San Diego youth soccer, I had crossed paths with almost all the parent/board members facing me. In the "heat of many battles" I had certainly "crossed swords" with a couple of them. Nevertheless, the cold, foreboding attitude of the board President gave me grave concern.

Eventually I was invited to speak. "I fully accept that referees have every reason to believe they should be treated with respect. The fact that I went over to the young man at the end of the game to apologize proves my "guilt." It also indicates genuine remorse since I had not received a Red Card at that time. In fact, at no time did I ever see a Red Card issued to me or was told that I was receiving a Red Card."

The board seemed confused by my explanation and stared at me, almost inviting me to continue.

"My main problem was not with the referee, but with the assistant referee who from the beginning was rude, antagonistic, and threatening." My words had "rung a bell." I had discovered between the game and the trial board how "infamous" this lady referee was. I continued,

"I have no excuses, only a sincere apology for my behavior and actions toward the referee. I was wrong and willingly accept whatever punishment the board gives me. The behavior of the assistant referee is no excuse on my behalf. I simply mention her because she bulldozed this poor young referee into giving me a Red Card long after the game was over. I truly don't know when, where, or how the Red Card was "shown" to me."

I spoke quietly, without force or rancor, not in any way trying to "win" this career threatening situation. I was asked to leave the room while the board discussed the matter, taking into account all the facts, including my explanation of the events of that fateful day. As I stood outside, I felt deflated, humble and fearful of what their decision may be. A lifetime ban or even extended ban from coaching would leave me out of soccer coaching. It suddenly hit me with full force how much my life depended not only on the money soccer coaching provided, but also the great joy, excitement, and reward of coaching talented, enthusiastic young soccer players; the camaraderie of working alongside other coaches, sharing experiences, telling jokes, and the thrill of game days and tournaments. Shortly, my future in youth soccer - maybe my life in San Diego and the USA - may be permanently impacted.

After a nerve wracking twenty minutes, I was called back in to face the trial board. I looked again into the faces of the members, trying to judge what the severity of the punishment may be. I looked at my "friendly" board member and saw a look of hope, if not joy.

"You will receive our decision in the mail within a few days," the President informed me in a clinical voice. "I will tell you clearly that had you come in here displaying any arrogance or trying to lay blame on the referee, you would have received the "ultimate punishment"," he informed me ominously.

I was totally deflated, feeling an incredible amount of anti-climax, not being given the decision there and then. I tried to hide my frustration, stood up, thanked all the board members, and also apologized for taking up so much of their time. I left the room and drove slowly to the Shakespeare English Pub near downtown to drown my sorrows and calm my nerves. I truly felt that my life was at a crucial crossroad, dependent on the decision of the trial board.

It was the decision of another board that was to cast my life into confusion and chaos.

The End of the Surf – The End of My Career?

A few days after my trial board, I drove to another pivotal meeting. This time it was with the board of the Surf Soccer Club, not really sure what I was going to face. I had high regard for all the board members and the professional way the Club was run. The Surf Club reputation was held in high regard nationally with its fantastic fields at the Polo Club and world renowned Surf Cup Tournament. The organization was strong and powerful. During my years working for the Club, I had made many great friends amongst the players and their parents. I was not naïve enough to believe that I had not angered or upset some of the Desperate Moms and Dads along the way. I was also my own worst enemy, commenting and giving opinions when asked (sometimes when not asked) on other coaches, players, and board members. Ironically, my old friend, Colin, had settled down well and had been promoted to head of the Surf Girls Soccer program. His progress, new found maturity, and professionalism, allied to his hard work and great soccer knowledge, were deservedly moving him up the ladder.

Despite many successes at the Surf, I was really a "square peg in a round hole." I acted and felt that I was one of the senior coaches, "leading" the Club, whereas I was in fact a lost soul. My divorce was final, and I spent most nights after training with my fellow coaches socializing when I did not have custody of my two sons.

When the meeting began, I was surprised and intimidated by the tone of the President when he spoke. There was no easy going bonhomie or friendliness as he spoke, calmly and directly. While setting out, accurately, my many successes and good work during my years at the Surf Club, he also balanced it fairly with negatives:

1. Altercation with the family at Presidio Cup,

2. Unacceptable behavior toward the former Club President at Audrey's regarding compensation for the Fundraiser Ball,

3. Certain arrogance beyond my coaching position with the Club,

4. Over opinionated,

5. Game day behavior on the sideline, especially toward referees,

6. The recent Red Card incident pending a decision

He delivered the pros and cons in an atmosphere of absolute quiet and an uncomfortable

pall fell on the room. Nobody there wished me any harm, and it was certainly no witch-hunt or backstabbing "coup."

It was time to move on for the Surf Club and Jeff Illingworth, was the crux of the President's speech. The fact that I had no other source of steady income, was facing a lengthy coaching ban, and had no money, made the timing of this conclusion disastrous. I would finish the season, thankfully, and would not return to the coaching staff of the Surf next season. Very fair and extremely professional.,

I was now waiting on a punishment from the trial board, and without any coaching position in the coming months. In the mid 1990's, there were still only a limited number of paid professional coaching jobs available. I had already burned my coaching opportunities at the two major youth soccer clubs – The Nomads and The Surf. Time to start looking in the mirror and figure out why I was able to build and develop youth soccer clubs. I had the adulation of my players and had coached many highly successful teams, yet finish close to the scrapheap.

I received the decision from the trial board banning me

from coaching the first six weeks of the following season, on game days only. It was bittersweet since an immediate ban on all my coaching would have meant an immediate end to my Surf coaching and cessation of income. Also, the following season was something that was a "million miles away" in that I had no coaching job arranged, nor any future prospects of one.

The future, in fact, looked very bleak as I pondered how to provide for my two sons, pay my rent, and survive.

15 years of Youth Coaching in the USA – All for Nothing?

Reflecting on the past 12 months was a dismal process. The loss of the La Jolla Lazers job was a surprising and crushing blow, followed by the car crash, Red Card, end of Surf job, and in the middle of the rest estate slump. I had arrived 15 years earlier in San Diego with a wife, no kids, $80,000, lots of energy, and a fearless approach to life. I had left behind in England two great careers, the rest of my family, two great soccer teams I enjoyed playing for, and a solid, successful life. Now, at 46 years of age, I had no wife, no money, no job, no car, two sons, and seemingly no future.

I realized with great clarity something that I had continually failed to understand about this rapidly exploding world of USA youth soccer. Ultimately, the pivotal, most important people were not the kids playing the game, nor the pro coaches being paid to coach them, nor the referees, despite their often misplaced feelings of self importance. Undoubtedly, it was the parents of these young soccer players who ultimately controlled the game. They were the ones who paid the fees for the Club to pay the coaches and buy uniforms and pay the referees. The parents were the ones who comprised the board of their children's soccer club. They would decide who was to coach in their club. The parents were the ones who would ultimately "graduate" to the higher, more important positions of power on the League and State boards. Even the referees were, in most cases, parents of youth soccer players.

In my arrogant, short sighted way, I had behaved for 15 years as though I was really important – "the star of the show."

My mind went back to my first Club, Mission Bay

Soccer Club and its "owner," Hank.

I had been forced out of there despite the thriving success of that Club. I had ignored the dire need to "keep all the parents happy." My mistakes, my bad; my desperate situation resulting from my ignorance or unwillingness to accept the importance and dire threat of an unhappy Desperate Soccer Mom or Dad!!!

Was there a way back for me in US youth soccer?

Should I pack up and return as a failure to England, turning my back on my two wonderful sons?

"It's only when you're at the bottom of the valley that you appreciate how great the view was from the top of the mountain." Sir Anthony Hopkins as President Nixon in the movie, Nixon.

THE END!!! Or was it???

Read – Desperate Soccer Moms and Dads – Part 2, coming soon to a soccer venue near you!

Before my girl's team played, I looked across the field and saw a parent watching the game whose face I recognized - Lionel Richie the famous singer. After the game he was signing autographs for some of my players. Jokingly I told him he better not sign up my players, or else! In response he asked if I was their coach. I told him I was writing a book "Desperate Soccer Moms (and Dads)." I asked him if he would be willing to take a photo with me to use in my book. I told him if the book was successful it could make him rich and famous. He was certainly NOT a desperate soccer dad by his behavior watching his daughter play. He had been calm, cool, and seated through out the game. A real gentleman.